BRITAIN IN OLD PHOTOGRAPHS

SWINDON

A SIXTH SELECTION

THE SWINDON SOCIETY

The
History
Press

LAST WEEK BUT ONE.

o

MAGIC PORTRAITS.

AMERICAN MAGIC
Photographic Likenesses
TAKEN DAILY AT
D. ABRAHAMS'S
PORTRAIT GALLERY,
MARKET-PLACE, SWINDON,
At the astonishing Reduced Charge from
1s. 6d. each and upwards.
Taken in any weather; sunshine is not rquired.

o

Think not these Portraits, by the light of Heaven made
Shades though they are, will like a shadow fade:
Know, when the lips of flesh and dust shall lie,
When Death's grey film o'erspreads the beaming eye,
These life-like Pictures, mocking at decay,
Will still be fresh and vivid as the day.

o

Every picture warranted to give entire satisfaction
and to stand the test of time and climate.

The Art taught. Apparatus and Chemicals supplied.

An interesting advertisement from 1856 for D. Abrahams's *American Magic Photographic Likenesses*, the Portrait Gallery, Market Place, Swindon. Notice the claim that the photographs could be taken in any weather – sunshine is not required! This pre-dates the earliest known Swindon photographic business which had been George King's (1859–76). It would appear that Abrahams was most likely a travelling photographer who stayed in the town for about two months, from December 1855 until the end of January 1856, residing at Bath Buildings before moving on again. The rapid advancement being made with photographic equipment can be gauged by the fact that by 1865 there were ten registered photographers in the town.

First published in 1998 by Sutton Publishing

Reprinted in 2012 by
The History Press
The Mill, Brimscombe Port,
Stroud, Gloucestershire, GL5 2QG
www.thehistorypress.co.uk

Copyright © The Swindon Society, 2012

Cover photographs. Front: William and Mary Hooper pictured outside their shop in Cromwell Street, 1912; *Back*: Swindon Town station platform in the 1940s; *Title page photograph*: William Hooper's shopfront, *c*. 1908.

British Library Cataloguing in Publication Data
A catalogue record for this book is available from the British Library.

ISBN 978-0-7509-1671-4

Typeset in 10/12 Perpetua.
Typesetting and origination by
Sutton Publishing Limited.
Printed and bound in England.

CONTENTS

A superb study of an early engine driver with his fireman on the footplate, pictured with the Works in the background.

INTRODUCTION

T he Swindon Society has once more delved into its archives to bring our readers another compilation of old photographs of Swindon. Since 1988, when the first volume was published (recently updated and re-issued, combined with the second selection, as *The Swindon Album*, in 1997, our twenty-fifth anniversary year), we have tried to interest local people in the history of the town through the medium of the photographer's art. Photographs used in these books date from 1847 to the 1980s for, as the motto of the Society states: 'History starts yesterday'.

For this sixth selection of photographs of Swindon, the vast majority of which have not been published before, the Society has continued with the format that has proved so successful in the previous five books. Included in its pages are scenes of Swindon people at work and at play, photographs of buildings now gone but still remembered, local personalities through the years, street scenes and events, both national and local, that have touched upon the lives of townsfolk through the years. We look back and marvel at the changes that have taken place since the 1830s, when the town's population was only about 1,700, to today when it is approaching 180,000. With the establishment of the new 'unitary' Borough of Swindon from 1 April 1997 we can look forward to the dawn of the Borough's second century and to the City status which could be the next milestone in our history.

In this book the camera has recorded views of local industries, including the great days of the Great Western Railway Works in the town when over 12,000 people were employed 'inside' the walls of the giant complex and almost everything in daily life depended on the railway. We have also included the many family businesses and shops which were the life-blood of the town in the years before the coming of the giant supermarket and commercial chainstores of the 1990s. Views of Swindon at war are included showing the volunteer services established during those traumatic years. Sporting and leisure activities are also covered together with some of the many arts and cultural societies that have flourished in the town for so many decades and which continue to do so today.

The work of local photographers is highlighted, with that of probably the most famous, William Hooper, having a section to itself. Hooper, who was born in the Cotswold village of Windrush, came to Swindon in the 1880s looking for employment in the GWR Works. He lost part of his right leg in an accident in the Works at the age of 22 and was forced to

The Baptist Social Union Football Club, pictured after becoming winners of the Swindon and District Free Church League in the 1906/7 season. This fine Protheroe & Simons photograph shows: (back row, left to right) A. Chatwin (Committee), G. McCrow (Captain), R. Padgett, F. Russell, F. Baldwin (Sec. BSU); (middle row) G.C. Dickson (Committee), c. Dymond, S. Waite, A.O. Turner, W. Ockwell, D. Ashby; (front row) F. Leighfield (Hon. Sec.), A. Rawlings, R. Lainchbury, W. Greenwood, H. Smith.

leave on medical advice. This led to William having to concentrate on his photography as a means of earning a living and, initially from a room in Merton Street and subsequently from shops in Market Street and Cromwell Street, he produced many of the most famous views of Swindon up to his retirement in 1921. Also, more of the perceptive and evocative views of Swindon and its inhabitants in the years since the Second World War taken by two of Hooper's successors, Denis Bird and Albert Beaney, are included in these pages.

In these years with the ever-changing face of Swindon, with its new estates, shopping centres, concrete and glass high-rise buildings, prestige office complexes and business parks, the Society hopes that its efforts will once again bring back many memories for local residents and encourage newcomers to the area to learn more of Swindon and its past. We would also be pleased to hear from anyone who would be interested in joining the Society as an active member as we look forward to the Millennium and another century. Contact Martin Vandervelde, Membership Secretary, 4 Lakeside, Swindon SN3 1QE.

CHAPTER ONE

OLD TOWN THROUGH THE YEARS

This photograph shows Isabella and Mrs Lay, outside their house, 48 Prospect Place, in 1930.

Marlborough Road, then called Coate Road, *c.* 1905. On the left is the embankment, near Evelyn Street, for the Midland and South Western Junction Railway, opened in 1881 as the Swindon, Marlborough and Andover Railway. The photograph was taken from near the junction of the present-day Lambourne Avenue.

Devizes Road, *c.* 1910. This peaceful scene, photographed by William Hooper and looking from the Newport Street junction, is now one of the main congested routes for traffic into Old Town.

A lovely Edwardian view of the rustic bridge in the Town Gardens, *c.* 1910. This is another picture from the Cromwell Street photographer William Hooper.

The Bandstand at the Town Gardens pictured in 1899. In the background can be seen the houses of Quarry Road. When the gardens were extended in 1905 an entrance was created from Quarry Road, along with a shelter and a maze (on the site of the present rose garden), both of which have since been removed.

The Bell and Shoulder of Mutton public house, 1 Marlborough Road, *c.* 1910. W.M. Mason was the proprietor during this period, and he advertised 'good stabling and loose boxes, good accommodation for cyclists etc.'. For a similar photograph just before closing as a pub in 1968, see *Swindon in Old Photographs IV*, p. 150. The building was demolished in 1969 by the Borough Council.

The Mall, looking north, *c.* 1930. This tree-lined street of large Edwardian terraced houses was built in the early years of the twentieth century. To the left can be seen the Commonweal School which was opened in 1927 as a secondary school with accommodation for 276 children.

St Margaret's Road, Old Town, looking towards Croft Road, *c.* 1910. The houses had been laid out on land owned by Levi Lapper Morse and named after his birthplace, Stratton St Margaret. The junction with Winifred Street is on the left.

A peaceful-looking Bath Road, *c.* 1904. The name that year had been changed from The Sands (a name used since the early nineteenth century), which was derived from the sandy nature of the soil around the Portland stone quarries nearby. This photograph, looking from near the entrance to Quarry Road, was taken by a local man whose identity is unknown except for the initials E.J.B.

A view of Church Farm, 1930s. The farmhouse was built using stone from Holy Rood Church when this was partly demolished in the 1850s (see *Swindon in Old Photographs I*, p. 11). Some of this material was again used, when the farm was demolished, to make the water feature etc. by the conservatories in Queens Park. The northern part of the Lawn estate was developed from 1954 in the fields of Church Farm. Churchfields School takes its name from the old homestead.

A photograph showing Christ Church in 1899, viewed from Drove Road. The church was originally built in 1851 to replace the over-crowded Holy Rood at the Lawns. The church was designed by Gilbert (later Sir Gilbert) Scott, who was also responsible for designing St Mark's at Church Place (in 1843) (see *Swindon in Old Photographs IV*, p. 75), the Martyrs' Memorial at Oxford, St Pancras station and the Albert Memorial in London.

Deacon's, the jeweller, watchmaker and china seller, shopfront, *c.* 1905. This business at 11–13 Wood Street, which was established in 1848, is still in existence today, selling the same quality items. In the 1930s Deacon's were also the agents for F.H. Ayres' sports goods, including tennis rackets as used by Fred Perry!

Keylock & Co., the butchers, 17 Wood Street, *c.* 1897. The display of meat on the trestles appears to include oxen. The premises are now occupied by Old Town Antiques. See also *Swindon in Old Photographs II*, p. 17.

Pictured outside his father's butcher's shop in Hythe Road in 1924 is John Slade. His mother Ida is showing concern that he remains firmly seated on the horse rather than looking at the photographer.

The shopfront of W.A. Slade, the family butchers at 1 Hythe Road, Old Town. The photograph shows a selection of the Christmas meats available in 1921. Pictured in the doorway are William and Ida Slade, with Jimmy Dunford and a boy called Dodson holding the delivery bicycles. William Slade later became a manager for the Co-op at Rodbourne Road. See p. 100 for a picture of William as Captain of Swindon Wednesday United Football Club.

The corner of Lethbridge Road and Croft Road, c. 1930. The building being demolished in the grounds of the house became a driving test centre for many years, and is now occupied by Countrywide Surveyors. To the left is the road bridge over the railway in Croft Road.

Townsends, solicitors, 42 Cricklade Street, 1950s. Originally built in 1729 for the Harding family, this building was acclaimed by the poet and writer, John Betjeman, in *Studies in the History of Swindon* (1950), as one of the most distinguished town houses in Wiltshire. Nikolaus Pevsner described it, in his book *Buildings of England – Wiltshire* (1963 & 1975), as the best house in Swindon by far. The owner of the property in 1811 was William Harding, and subsequent owners are said to be John Villet, Robert Harding, Thomas Morse and William Villet. A William Jenner became the owner in 1854 but later it had multiple occupation for many years. Up to 1898 Messrs Townsend and Jones, solicitors, occupied the first floor, with a firm of estate agents, probably Adams, sharing the ground floor with the entire tax inspectorate of Swindon. James Coplestone Townsend (1825–85) was also Solicitor to the Swindon, Marlborough & Andover Railway (later MSWJR) and Board Meetings of the SM&AR were held in 42 Cricklade Street in the 1870s. The building was also the office of the Secretary of the Railway Company, Charles Brooke, at this time. The house is of five bays and two storeys with a mixture of brick and stone. The large grotesque keystone heads above the window are notable. Inside is a fine staircase. Some of the stonework on top of the roof, including the urn shown in this view, was removed for safety reasons shortly after this photograph was taken. A history of Townsends, from the eighteenth century to date, was compiled by Graham Young in 1966. For a view of Cricklade Street and Townsends in 1906, see *Swindon in Old Photographs* (*The Swindon Album*), p. 22.

This was the view looking along Wood Street from the junction of Victoria Road and Bath Road, April 1953. To the left is an old building known locally as 'The Manor House', about which little is known. This building was demolished in the 1960s to allow Queen Victoria House to be built.

The junction of Wood Street and Devizes Road, 1950s. Dentry's, the tailors, occupied the site which today is Charles Harding, the estate agents. Note the cycle propped up against the kerb – a common sight in those more innocent days.

The shopfront of J.A. Workman & Sons, 49 Prospect Place, 1968. Among the special offers advertised in the window are Cheddar cheese at 3s 4d per lb and Welsh butter at 3s per lb. The shop is still in business today.

The Fountain public house, Devizes Road, 1968. Built in 1847 as the Britannia, on the corner of Britannia Place, it was renamed the Fountain when it was extended in 1870. It was used by Swindon Town FC as their dressing rooms when home matches were played at the Croft (on the site of the present St Margarets Road) in the 1890s. In recent years it has been renamed the Hobgoblin after modernization by the Wychwood Brewery.

Masons' Arms Hotel, 29–31 High Street, 1965. The premises were sold to Swindon Borough Council in July 1969, and subsequently demolished to permit road widening. The Midland Bank building stands approximately on the site of part of this old inn.

Quantock Motors, 4 and 5 Devizes Road, 1961. They were the local agents for Standard cars. In the foreground are vehicles from Swindon School of Motoring, with a Standard 8,10, Pennant, and a Triumph Herald on the end. The Herald was the first of this model in Wiltshire, having been delivered under wraps direct from the Motor Show. The site was later occupied by Barclays Bank, and now by the DPDS Consulting group.

E. Smith, butchers, 4 High Street, 1975. The building was formerly a public house of some ill repute, the King of Prussia – well known for fighting and prostitution. The premises were closed in 1880 and subsequently became a well-known local butcher's shop (for a view in c. 1910 see Swindon in Old Photographs III, p. 38). This unique building was sadly demolished in 1981 and a superficially similar office block, Eastcott House, was built on the site.

Swindon Town station platform on a busy day in the 1940s. The station, situated off Newport Street, was built by the Swindon, Marlborough & Andover Railway for north–south traffic and opened in 1881. The small cross-country line became the Midland & South Western Junction Railway (MSWJR) in 1884. The station, built close to the cattle market, initially had two platforms but was enlarged in 1904–5 by making the Up platform into an island. It was the second largest station on the MSWJR system, with over 1,500 ft of platform faces. One regular duty for station staff in the halcyon days of the MSWJR before the First World War was the release of racing pigeons sent down from northern England. On one Saturday in June 1909 a record total of 80,000 birds were sent off from Swindon Town! Also in those days, on Lifeboat Day every year, a boat would arrive at the station and be drawn in procession on a wagon of six horses to be floated on Beatrice Street lake – see *Swindon in Old Photographs* (*The Swindon Album*), pp. 144–5. The Down platform also had a fine garden, situated below the company offices (later the headquarters of the Marlborough–Swindon Camp Club – see *Swindon in Old Photographs V*, p. 96). During the First World War the line carried an immense amount of military traffic north and south – this was to be repeated in the Second World War. During both conflicts it was a vitally important strategic route for the war effort. The MSWJR was taken over by the GWR under the Railways Act of 1923 and passenger traffic continued to the station until closure under British Railways in September 1961. Day excursions had continued directly through to towns on the south coast (such as Bournemouth) until the closure. Some coal and oil traffic continued until 1966 and 1968 respectively. The buildings were demolished in 1968 after suffering fire damage. During 1970–1, however, the Old Town station site saw a brief resurgence of life as the off-loading point for trainloads of stone from the Mendip quarries, destined, ironically enough, for construction of the M4 motorway. The last passenger train to run into the station site was probably the Locomotive Club of Great Britain's *Somerset Quarryman* tour in April 1972. Today the site is the Central Trading Estate, with light industry units. For further views of the station see *Swindon in Old Photographs* (*The Swindon Album*), pp. 126 & 60–3, and V, pp. 18–19. Also see pp. 24, 133 & 156 of this volume.

Swindon Town (Old Town) station refreshment rooms, *c.* 1933. The licence was first granted in 1894 and the bar remained virtually unaltered, with gas lighting, potted palms, Victorian beer handles, ornately carved tables and a 1904 till that would only ring up a total of 2s 11d, until closure on 1 February 1965. It was known locally as the Ghost Train after passenger services ceased in 1961. Note the poster on the left advertising a show at the Empire Theatre.

Tom Salmon from the BBC West television programme interviewing some of the regulars at the last day of opening of the Ghost Train (Swindon Town station refreshment rooms), 1 February 1965. Among the regulars was Bill Cutler (second from the right), a renowned breeder of Staffordshire bull terrier dogs, several of which became Crufts champions. He was also chauffeur to R. Bowley of Bowley's Brewery, Old Town. Between the men can be seen the 1904 till.

Another view of the last Old Town Fair to be held in High Street, 1965. The sign of the Bell Hotel against the sky gives a perfect setting to this photograph. The building with its present frontage was built in 1800, although the carving over the entrance is dated 1515 for the establishment of the original building. Its original name was the Lapwing, and besides having been a posting house for mail coaches to London, it was also the site of the first post office in the town. Now in the process of being revamped, the restaurant area has recently been renamed Fusion!

The last Old Town Fair, High Street, September 1965. See *Swindon in Old Photographs I*, p. 140, for another photograph of this fair. Later it moved to the County Ground car park, but after resurfacing of the parking area and the concerns of local residents, it has had to relocate again.

Mechanical Office Equipment Ltd shop, 96 Victoria Road, 1968. These premises are in the block below Newspaper House – see *Swindon in Old Photographs III*, p. 26. At this time it still retained its original porchway and street number (no. 16). It is now greatly altered and is the premises of Nature's Larder.

Downs View Road in the early 1950s. This was one of a series of photographs that were used to show the benefits of moving to Swindon at the time, describing these houses as examples of private purchase available.

The Vintner, off licence, 25 High Street, 1965. On the end of the Old Town Hall, adjacent to the Market Square, this old building was once owned by John Jefferies, grandfather of the author Richard Jefferies. It was demolished in the early 1970s to allow road widening to take place.

CHAPTER TWO

THE RAILWAY WORKS
& SYSTEM

This group of GWR men had just completed the Improvement Class for Enginemen and Firemen at Swindon in 1911. Unfortunately we have no record of their names. The photograph was taken by Arthur Banbury of Faringdon Street, Swindon.

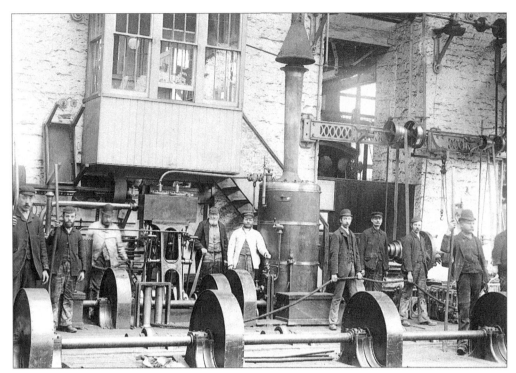

This fine interior photograph within the GWR shows men working in 'G' shop in the early part of the twentieth century. Pictured from the left are ? Boulton, *c.* Whately, H. Blake, W. Bullock, J. Cook, G. Gosling, J. Linton, J. Knox, J. Brown and H. Hinder. William Hooper, being an ex-employee, must have obtained special permission to take photographs within the complex.

An unusual view taken by Hooper in about 1910 from the roof-top of the Junction station, on the Down track side, i.e. the Bristol line side (which is of course now demolished). Outside the coal wharf can be seen the laden wagons awaiting unloading, while in the background are Sheppard Street and Gloucester Street.

This picture will evoke many happy memories for generations of young Swindon train-spotters. Hooper has captured everything about the GWR in this picture of the station, *c.* 1920. Outside the headline-grabbing express trains on the main lines, every day hundreds of journeys were made transporting heavy goods trains across the region, moving essentials for the large industrial towns.

A further view of the Fitting Shop in the Carriage and Wagon Department, *c.* 1907. This is another picture from the series taken in the Works by the Swindon photographer William Hooper, who had himself been an employee 'inside' until he was injured in a serious accident.

Inside the GWR Works, *c.* 1907, showing a section of the Fitting Shop in the Carriage and Wagon Department. The noise from all the machines must have been terrible for the men working there. This is one of a series of photographs taken by William Hooper, the Swindon photographer.

This lovely Hooper photograph shows the Royal Train, drawn by 'Star' class locomotive No. 4041 *Prince of Wales*, on 14 July 1903, carrying King Edward VII, passing through Swindon on a record run between Paddington and Plymouth. The journey time was four and a half hours, and the train passed through Swindon at 11.47 a.m. as opposed to the scheduled time of 11.59 a.m.

This shows No. 111 *The Great Bear* in pristine condition in an official photograph taken by William Hooper. When built in February 1908 to a design by G.J. Churchward, it became the only 4–6–2 locomotive ever built by the GWR. Its weight of 97 tons 5 cwt meant that, with such a heavy axle loading, it was restricted to the Paddington to Bristol line working only. When it was due to be re-boilered in September 1924, C.B. Collett made the decision to rebuild it as a 4–6–0 'Castle' class locomotive. Following its conversion it retained the same number but acquired the name *Viscount Churchill* from locomotive No. 2975, which in turn became Sir Ernest Palmer.

No. 4021 *King Edward* pictured in exactly the same position within the Works. This 'Star' class locomotive was built in June 1909 at Swindon to a 4–6–0 design by G.J. Churchward and weighed 75 tons 12 cwt. It lost its name in June 1927 with the advent of the King class and was renamed *The British Monarch*, which was amended again to *British Monarch* in October 1927. When built it was fitted with the 'No. 3 Swindon superheater', which from this time became the standard fitment for future engines.

A lovely pen and ink cartoon of 'Trip' morning by Will Thomas, the local artist. The first of the trains departed from the Works in the early hours of the morning. See *Swindon in Old Photographs IV*, p. 20, and V, p. 32, for more examples of cartoons of 'Trip' week.

Another cartoon by Will Thomas on the events that took place in Swindon the week after the 'Trip' holidays. This shows the local traders such as the butcher, baker and grocer, along with the rent collector, attempting to get payment. It was not until 1938 that the railway workers actually received holiday pay.

Pictured outside the Erecting Shop at the GWR Works, Swindon in 1935 are *King George V* (6000) and the reconstructed early locomotive *North Star*. The latter was rebuilt for the centenary of the Stockton & Darlington Railway in 1925 and used some of the original items 'found' stored around the Works. It was removed from its normal home in 'A' Shop for the centenary of the GWR in 1935 and used for promotional work, including being used in the film *Romance of a Railway*. *King George V* had been constructed within the Works by June 1927, and was used for exhibition purposes within the region. In August 1927 it was shipped from Cardiff docks to the USA to take part as the British representative at the Centenary Celebration of the Baltimore and Ohio Railroad Company, which was called 'The Fair of the Iron Horse'. During this event it had the honour of leading the procession of modern locomotives. As a souvenir of these celebrations, the engine was presented with its now famous bell with the inscription: 'Presented to locomotive *King George V* by the Baltimore and Ohio Railway Company in commemoration of its Centenary Celebration Sept. 24th–Oct. 15th 1927'. Along with the bell, replicas were cast of a gold medal also presented at the event; these were placed either side of the cab. The engine returned late in November from the show, and by December was back on regular service within the region. When the GWR was nationalised in 1948 the engine had already completed over a million miles on the tracks. It was withdrawn from service in November 1962 and stored at Swindon. During 1968 it was restored to working order for H.P. Bulmers Ltd (the cider makers), who put it on display at their Hereford factory. When British Rail relaxed its rules on main line steam running, the engine made a comeback, running special excursions for enthusiasts until 1987 when its main line boiler certificate expired. Since then a 6000 Locomotive Association took custody of the engine hoping to restore it to main line running. This proved not to be possible, and the engine has since been used for exhibition purposes only. In 1992 it moved to the Railway Museum in Faringdon Road as a replacement for Lode Star which was returned to York. See *Swindon in Old Photographs II*, p. 57, for a picture of *King George V* at the exhibition in the USA.

GWR Works on 20 May 1921, showing 'W' Shop and Joe Claridge and his gang of apprentice fitters and turners. The only person identified is Joe Claridge himself, who is fourth from the right, wearing a cap and a tie.

Pictured beside an engine on a trial at Dauntsey Bank in 1927 are the driver and fireman with Chargeman A. Drinkwater. Outside his work for the GWR, Drinkwater was a councillor and became the Mayor of Swindon in 1943–4. See *Swindon in Old Photographs V*, p. 139, for a further picture of him on official duties.

This photograph outside the Mechanics' Institute, *c.* 1935, shows the Great Western Railway Swindon Staff Gleemen. During this period the group made a broadcast on the radio which was well received in the town, as well as a record with the tunes 'Allan Water' and 'John Peel'. Back row, left to right: P. Harris, Jack Parker, Gordon Bond, Charlie Ireland, T. Beasant, A. Davis, J. Witts; middle row: T. Summerhayes, W. Williams, *c.* Gee, W. Watts, A. Middleton, F. Reynolds, H. Axton, F. Hook, T. Lawrence, P. Pearce, L. Whipp; front row: W. Gunter, A. Fowler, A. Russell, Jack Winter (Conductor), J. Kelynack (President), W. Bartlett, *c.* West (accompanist), H. Nash.

Pictured in the GWR Works in the 1950s is Cecil Harvey, who is working in a refurbished carriage putting the final touches to the french polishing.

Looking across Ferndale Road recreation ground towards the GWR gasworks buildings (near Harcourt Road) in the 1950s. At this plant they produced only small coke. In the foreground can be seen the fence which marks the edge of the old North Wilts Canal.

Looking across the main railway tracks towards the Gypsy Lane gasworks, 1965. This photograph has a very atmospheric feeling of times past.

A photograph of the gleaming steam locomotive 2–10–0 No. 92220 *Evening Star* pictured in the Works on 23 November 1960. Outshopped on 18 March 1960, this was the last steam locomotive built for British Railways.

A view of the Locomotive Erecting Shop in the Railway Works, February 1960. In the foreground are the new diesel-hydraulic locomotives ('Warship' class) being built, including No. D804 *Avenger*, while in the background can be seen steam engines under repair, including No. 5024 *Carew Castle*.

Diesel-hydraulic locomotives under construction in the 'A' Erecting Shop, February 1959. This shop had been built in 1923 by the GWR originally to build steam locomotives, but by this period the newly constructed work-bay was involved in the manufacture of the first diesel-hydraulic locomotives ('Warship' D800 class, of which thirty-eight were built).

Pictured working in No. 19 Shop (known as 'The Klondike' by the workers) in 1969 is Dave Skeates, whose job was shampooing and cleaning the seat covers removed from the coaches while in the Works for repair.

A most unusual photograph which will bring back memories for many people associated with working 'inside' (within the Works). This shows the old-style washbasins on the locomotive side. These remained in use until the closing of the Works.

British Rail Engineering Ltd.

SWINDON WORKS

Open Day

September 7th 1974.

CONDITIONS OF ISSUE

The Company will not be responsible for the death of or injury to any person exercising the permission given by this permit whilst on the Company's premises, nor for any loss of or damage to the property of any such person howsoever such death, injury, loss or damage may be caused, and whether or not by the act, neglect or default of the Company, their servants or agents.

The taking of photographs for private use is permitted. Those for commercial purposes must be submitted for approval prior to publication.

A card issued by British Rail Engineering Ltd, on the open day at the Works, 7 September 1974. Among the events organized were three different routes visitors could take around the Works (fifty-seven stands), events such as skittles, a flower show, rifle-shooting competitions, a long-distance balloon race and a photographic competition on *King George V*, which was pulling coaches within the Works.

Demolition in progress on a section of Swindon station, June 1972. Part of the old platform can be seen. The original GWR station was built by Messrs J. & c. Rigby of Millbank, London, and opened in 1842. When the original plans were published in April 1972 for the alterations and the building of an office complex, the cost had been estimated at one million pounds.

Another view of the demolition in progress at Swindon station, June 1972. In the foreground can be seen the original tunnels countless passengers over the years have used to reach the platforms. In the background are the main railway works.

CHAPTER THREE

STREETS, SHOPS, SERVICES & BUSINESS

A busy scene with pedestrians shopping at Regent Circus in the 1950s. In the centre of the picture are the premises of Maybury's the printers, famous in the early part of the twentieth century for their postcard views of Swindon.

This very early photograph shows the shopfront of John Hill, butchers, in 1873, with his Christmas meat display. John Hill is standing behind the trestle table. The shop was at 38 Bridge Street (the site now of the Britannia Building Society).

The shopfront of 14 Fleet Street, showing the sign of Charlie Hill, 'the Workingman's Butcher', in 1934. Pictured on the extreme right is Charlie Hill (senior), while next to him is Charlie Hill (junior). The shop was not very successful, partly because customers wouldn't cross the busy road to shop, even with enticements such as a free $^1/_4$ lb of boiled sweets when you purchased a certain amount of meat.

This excellent Fred Viner photograph shows road works taking place outside the shops in Fleet Street, c. 1912. The shopfront of C.M. Hill (the family butcher) is shown, the shop on the extreme right being another butcher's, Frank Bailey at no. 45, while on the left of Hill's was a breadshop, then a further butcher's, Horace Drury (no. 44). At the end of the block was Edgington's, the out-door beerhouse and bottling plant. The young boy standing by the horses and wearing a white hat is Charlie Hill (junior).

This unusual photograph from 1926 shows part of the old slaughterhouse in Eastcott Hill, next to the Duke of Wellington public house. It shows a young Charlie Hill being held on the animal by the drover, Zonk Thorne. Also in the picture is Stan Heath (holding the animal's head) and, on the extreme right, Charlie Hill (junior).

Outside the Co-operative Confectionery Department shop at 16 Fleet Street, *c.* 1919. The only members of staff identified so far are Miss Sutton (first on the right) and, next to her, Florence Haines (Manageress). See p. 59 for another picture of Miss Haines as an assistant at Rodbourne Road Branch No. 2 shop. This photograph was taken by the Swindon photographers Protheroe & Simons.

This photograph of the corner house in Merton Street at the junction with Turl Street, *c.* 1890, shows Thomas Hacker and his family, who ran the business of bread, flour, corn and meal stores from the rear of the premises. The business of corn and potato merchants was later transferred to Corporation Street, which Jack and Henry Hacker ran, with two sisters (Betty and Edith Hacker) looking after the little shop.

The Golden Lion public house, 43 Bridge Street, *c.* 1910. The pub was situated on the junction with the Wilts and Berks Canal, and was noted for a magnificent sculpture of a lion which was set on the parapet above the door. During this period it was owned by the Cirencester Brewery Company. Later the lion was removed and placed on a plinth alongside the canal: see *Swindon in Old Photographs II*, p. 133. The pub was closed in 1956 and subsequently demolished, and the licence transferred to the Southbrook Inn.

A view looking up Regent Street, July 1918. Soldiers are constructing an embankment and relaying the tramcar lines after the demolition of the Golden Lion canal bridge. To the right is the Golden Lion public house. For another view, see *Swindon in Old Photographs I*, p. 93, and also *III*, pp. 77–9, for the bridge in its heyday.

Bridge Street, *c.* 1925. Tramcar No. 13 has just reached the passing loop having departed from the Centre on its way to Old Town and the Corn Exchange. The advertisement on the tram is for Hyslop's the optician. Built in 1921, tramcar No. 13 is still in existence today, but is in a dilapidated condition in a barn near Purton awaiting funds for renovation. See also *Swindon in Old Photographs I*, p. 94.

Regent Street, looking up towards the McIlroys tower, *c.* 1910, with a tram heading towards the centre. Above the driver can be seen an advertisement for 'Greenaway's Boots'. Among the many shop signs are Rydill's the publishers (on the left), the firm which produced many of the early Swindon postcards, with the Public Benefit Boot Company next door. On the right is an ornate gas lamp outside the Fox Tavern on the corner with Cromwell Street. This postcard was published by John Drew of Swindon.

Looking towards the Whitehouse public house, Station Road, *c.* 1920. The name was changed from the Queens Arms in 1910. Usher's Brewery took over as owners in 1918. The premises, which had been empty for a period, have recently been reopened with an Irish theme, simulating the atmosphere of a typical Irish pub.

The imposing shopfront of The Retlaw Cycle Co., 41 Faringdon Road, which was situated on the corner with Farnsby Street. It was owned by Walter (Retlaw spelt backwards) Slocombe and traded through the 1920s until 1937, when the premises were incorporated into Rye and Blackwell, the ironmongers, who had traded nearby for a number of years. Besides bicycles, they stocked tyres, plugs, and lamps; they also sold gramophones, records, etc. In the right-hand shop window can be seen a large display of Meccano, which must have been a big attraction to the local boys at the time.

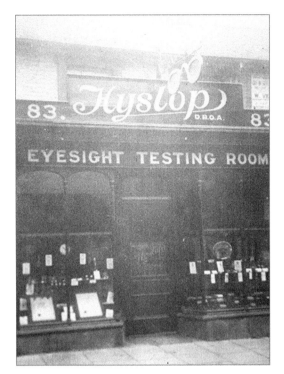

The shopfront of Hyslop's at 83 Regent Street, *c*. 1920. Notice the large sign with a pair of ornate spectacles showing the premises to be an optician's. Today the site of this shop is occupied by New Look. Established by Mr S.R. Hyslop in 1904, the business still trades today as Hyslop & Leighton in Wood Street, Old Town.

The premises of W.H. Smith & Son, 53 Fleet Street, 1930. It was opened in 1925, when they purchased the premises of T. Hullin, bookseller and newsagent. They continued trading here until the new, larger store was opened in Regent Street in 1973, although the firm had been contemplating the move as early as 1959.

Kingshill Co-operative Society Bakery, 54 Radnor Street, 1906. This new bakery opened that year and also included a stable alongside, with three stalls and a loose box. When built it was said to be the most up-to-date and convenient bakery in the town. The site is now occupied by Beds Direct warehouse and showrooms.

Kingshill Co-operative Society bakery – an interior view of the bakehouse and ovens, etc., 1906. The bakehouse was 48 ft by 33 ft with two steam drawplate ovens, each capable of baking 200 loaves. A mixing and bread-making room was on the floor above, with a flour store on the top floor. The walls of the bakehouse were lined from floor to ceiling with white glazed bricks.

Pictured outside their Cromwell Street headquarters in 1935 are Captain Baker and the staff of the Swindon Borough Fire Brigade. The only people identified so far are Fireman Sylvester (extreme left) and, next to him, Fireman Wilf Hedges. Note the names on the Dennis engines, 'Lassie' and 'Laddie', although the Morris Commercial on the right is un-named. 'Lassie', the smaller of the two Dennis engines, was used for county calls while 'Laddie' was reserved for town work. In 1935 new Cromwell fire helmets were purchased for the fifteen firemen on the staff and the Brigade was the first in the west of England to be provided with Rutco leather fire tunics. Captain Baker retired in March 1938 after 20 years' service in the Brigade.

The story of the fire service in Swindon dates back to the mid-nineteenth century. Old Town had a fire engine at least as far back as 1853 – a horse-drawn Shand Mason manual pump, with room for the crew to ride, which is now in Bath Road Museum. In New Town, around 1870, the Great Western Railway made their steamer pump available to the townsfolk for any fires that occurred. The Old Town fire engine was kept in Newport Street in 1864 with the keys being available at the police station and by a Mr W. Read. The appliance was also available for hire in surrounding towns and villages when necessary. It was used at Wootton Bassett in 1867 and Cricklade in 1868 for a fee of 2 guineas. At this time fires were fought by any volunteers willing or available at the scene, but in November 1879 a Volunteer Fire Brigade was established. The engine had initially been housed in Newport Street; later, however, fire stations were built at the Sands (Bath Road) end of the Quarries and in Lansdown Road. When the new Town Hall was built in 1891, in view of the forthcoming amalgamation of the Old and New Town Boards into the Swindon Borough Council, it included a fire station on its north side. Original plans show double doors in the first bay of brickwork outside the delivery entrance with the legend 'Fire Station' above. This is now infilled with windows and brickwork. The Cromwell Street fire station was built in 1901 and used until 1959, when a new headquarters was built by the roundabout at the County Road/Drove Road junction. For other views of the Fire Brigade in the early years of the twentieth century, see *Swindon in Old Photographs IV*, pp. 111–12.

Here in the yard at the Cromwell Street fire station in 1938 is regular Fireman Sylvester (extreme right), who is giving instructions on the workings of a 125 gpm trailer pump.

This imposing building was 1 Bridge Street, at the junction with Station Road, 1960s. During this period it was the headquarters of the local Communist party and posters can be seen requesting votes for Ike Gradwell, the local candidate, who was also the local secretary of the party.

The premises of S.J. Haskins, decorator, 126 Commercial Road, *c.* 1930. The business had used these premises for a number of years during the 1920s and '30s, and later it became the office for the Wesleyan and General Assurance Society. The Sun Alliance Insurance Group used the premises until recently, but the present occupants are Winslow Bros, the local financial services company.

An evocative view of Swindon's past, the Market Café, pictured in 1968. This was the regular meeting place for both traders and shoppers. Prices ranged from 6*d* for tea, to assorted minerals at 10*d*, cheese and onion rolls at 10*d*, and cheese and ham rolls at 1s. For other interior views of the old market during this period, see *Swindon in Old Photographs IV*, p. 144.

The shopfront of W. Waite, wholesale and retail tobacconists, 34 Milton Road, 1965. The premises are now occupied by Frilsons Insurance Services.

Pictured on the premises of Great Western Clothiers in Faringdon Road in 1963 is the Mayor of Swindon (Councillor Arthur E. Cockram), being advised on suitable material for a suit. Dennis Morris (left) is being helped by one of his assistants. Over the years many of the previous holders of the position of mayor had been customers of the shop.

A window display at the Evening Advertiser offices, Victoria Road, 1938. The exhibition was to advertise a new range of raincoats available for sale at Great Western Clothiers' store in Faringdon Road.

The Great Western Clothiers' stand at the Bath & West Show, Broome Manor, 4 June 1957. The stand had been hastily assembled by the staff using any available material at the last minute. Pictured at the stand is Dennis Morris (on the right), along with one of his assistants.

Dennis and Sylvia Morris, the owners of Great Western Clothiers, pictured outside their store just prior to its closure in October 1987. The shop had originally opened in 1899, and had prided itself that generations of the same families had always shopped there. Dennis had started work there as an apprentice in 1942, at wages of 15s per week, before becoming a partner and later taking over the business. These premises are now occupied by Giggles Costume Hire and Cotswold Sewing Machines.

CHAPTER FOUR

EVEN SWINDON,
GORSE HILL, MOREDON
& RODBOURNE CHENEY

The mural of George and the Dragon, Manton Street, Rodbourne, 1975. It was based on Uccello's panel in the National Gallery of St George killing the dragon, and was the first of a series of murals organized by the Thamesdown Community Arts. It was later repainted in the 1980s, after complaints by local residents concerned about the poor condition of the painting. This was to no avail as the buildings were later demolished in the redevelopment of the area.

The premises of A. Jones, The Even Swindon Bakery, 40 Jennings Street, *c.* 1905. The major part of the building can be seen spreading along Rose Street. Mr Jones owned the premises for a number of years from the turn of the century. In 1926 Wilfred Castle took them over, which was the start of a number of Castle bread shops around Swindon; at its height just before the last war there were seven shops and two bakehouses. The last premises in Market Street were sold in October 1997 to Mountstevens Ltd.

The Rodbourne Cheney post office and general stores, pictured in Moredon Road at the junction with Church Walk South, *c.* 1915. It was owned by G.B. Lewis during this period, and is now the site of the Gateway supermarket.

Rodbourne Road, Rodbourne, *c.* 1916, showing the frontage of the New Swindon Industrial Co-operative Society Branch No. 2 (still in use today as a Co-op shop). The people standing outside in this William Hooper photograph are, from left to right, Bert Saunders (Senior Apprentice), Arthur Parry (Junior Apprentice), D. Brockley (assistant), T.J. Langcaster (Branch Manager) and Florence Haines (assistant). See *Swindon in Old Photographs IV*, p. 95 and V, p. 50, for other groups of Co-op workers outside the same shop.

Rodbourne Road, Rodbourne, *c.* 1916, this time showing the interior of the Co-op shop. Once again the staff are Florence Haines (assistant), D. Brockley (assistant), Arthur Parry (Junior Apprentice), T.J. Langcaster (Branch Manager) and Bert Saunders (Senior Apprentice). Among the adverts on display are those for CWS cocoa, Family Jars that promote 'Harmony in the Home', and a slogan: 'our teas – full weight without the wrapper'. This is another William Hooper photograph.

Rodbourne, looking across waste land towards Even Swindon School and the Church Hall in Romsey Street in the early 1970s. The land has since been built on and forms part of Alfred Bown Court (opened 17 September 1976, and named after A.J. Bown MBE, who was Mayor of Swindon 1968–9 and Freeman of the Borough).

A view of Bruce Street railway bridge during rebuilding work in July 1956, to allow the passage of double-decker buses. It has been rebuilt again in recent years for road widening and the creation of new traffic islands.

Children of Wembley Street and Iffley Road watching a Punch and Judy Show during the celebrations for the Coronation of King George VI and Queen Elizabeth, 1937.

Children from Richmond Road playing snowballs in the fields, 1949. This area is now part of the site of St Mary's Roman Catholic School in Bessemer Road. The houses in the background are part of Churchward Avenue. Left to right: Terry Harvey, Clive Herbert, Alan Harvey, Trevor Holliday, David Powell, Lennard Harvey, Margaret Marshman, Douglas Stewart, Brian Harvey. This is yet another of the many photographs from the camera of Albert Beaney, see *Swindon in Old Photographs V*, p.123.

Cricklade Road, Gorse Hill on 24 May 1937. These local children are dressed in fancy costumes celebrating Empire Day. Among those identified are Margaret Fowler, Cathleen Fowler, Molly Nurden, Maurice Palmer, ? Nurden, the Grub brothers and Mrs Hewer. In the background can be seen the shop of E.F. Steele (no. 16) and the saddler's shop of H.W.J. Tuck.

Argyle Street, Gorse Hill, again on the occasion of Empire Day, 24 May 1937. Identified are Margaret Fowler, Edna and Eileen Gilman, Pam Wilson, Jean Smith, Molly Nurden and her sister (?), the Grub brothers and Cyril (?) Cox.

Castle Combe mural on the end wall of a house in Cricklade Road, 1976. Painted by the 17th Swindon (St Barnabas') Scout Troop, with the assistance of the Thamesdown Community Arts, it lasted until 1985, when a new owner of the property painted out this landmark owing to a misunderstanding.

The Moonrakers pub in Cricklade Road, 1950s. When it opened in 1953 it became the first public house premises to be granted a new licence in Swindon since the Rodbourne Arms in 1905. It had been built originally in 1931 as the Crossways Club.

Moredon Power Station, with a locomotive on the ex-MSWJR line to Cricklade, 1960s. The power station was taken out of use in 1973 and demolished in 1979; it is now the site of Pembroke Park housing estate. See also *Swindon in Old Photographs V*, pp. 53 and 55.

An idyllic scene in 1935, with a seating area at Rodbourne Green. In the background is the Manor House.

Looking down Moredon Road, with the Boys' Brigade marching to parade on a Sunday morning, 1960s.

Rodbourne Cheney, a view looking north from the tower of St Mary's Church, 1935. Behind the houses in Cheney Manor Road can be seen only allotments and fields. Note also the corporation single-decker bus which has just departed from the Rodbourne Arms.

Once again a view from the tower of St Mary's Church, but this time looking towards the newly built Vicarage Road, see *Swindon in Old Photographs IV*, p. 69. Across the fields in this 1935 photograph can be seen the Iffley Road gas holders on the edge of the old North Wilts Canal.

CHAPTER FIVE

CHURCHES, CHAPELS
& SCHOOLS

St Saviour's Church, Ashford Road, c. 1910. The church was built by local voluntary labour (mostly GWR employees and parishioners of St Mark's) in 1889. When enlarged again in 1904, the volunteers included the Bishop of Bristol (Dr Forrest Browne). The old wooden church was clad in stone and rededicated by the Bishop of Malmesbury in 1961.

Looking down a section of Cheney Manor Road towards St Mary's Church at Rodbourne Cheney at the beginning of the twentieth century. In front of the church can be seen the allotments that had been in use for many years.

An interior view looking east towards the altar of St Mary's Church, Rodbourne Cheney, *c.* 1913. The photograph was produced for postcard sale by an unknown publisher.

St Paul's Church, Edgeware Road, *c.* 1910. The church had been built in 1881, and was finally demolished in 1965 for extensions to the Woolworth's store. For an interior view of the church, see *Swindon in Old Photographs IV*, p. 79.

The nave and chancel of Holy Rood Catholic Church, Groundwell Road, *c.* 1913. The church had been opened in 1905. For an early exterior view, see *Swindon in Old Photographs II*, p. 76.

A rare photograph of Canon Harvey's sister (on the left) and his wife posing for the camera. See p. 71 for details on Canon Harvey.

Sanford Street Congregational Church Junior Choir, *c.* 1924/5, outside the church. Among those identified are, back row: ? Mittens, Margaret Whiting, Donald Whiting, Biddy Wiltshire, Phil Clarcy, Doris Saunders, Joan Ludlow; middle row: Mr Bullock, Mr Wiltshire, Myfanwy Johns, Mrs Bullock (conductor), Revd J. Simon, Mrs Johns (pianist), Mr Bright; front row: May Miles, Sidney Sheldon, Barbara Whiting, Billie Bullock, Nora Mittens, John Jervis.

A portrait of Canon Henry Bache Harvey BA, who was at St Augustine's Church in Rodbourne for twenty-nine years. He was born in 1863 and ordained a Deacon in 1886. From 1888 to 1895 Canon Harvey was the vicar at Palmerston in New Zealand, before returning as curate at Twerton in Bath. From 1902, when the church district of Rodbourne was set up, he was installed as vicar. His first task was to raise funds for a parish church, as only a small mission room was available for use at this time. There was a site for a church but it was in use as allotments. At first he managed to raise a small amount of funds to build a chancel on to the Mission Room, which made it look more like a church. Luckily for Rodbourne people, Canon Harvey possessed a share in the Great Western Railway. This allowed him a copy of the shareholders' names and addresses to whom he wrote letters of appeal. With the help of friends 32,000 letters were dispatched, all handwritten, and this raised over £3,800. Among other schemes was the sale of 'penny bricks' (similar to the recent Prospect brick appeal) and after much hard work the church was completed and dedicated on St Paul's Day, 25 January 1908.

Canon Harvey died on 28 May 1931 at Glenwood Nursing Home, Swindon. It was reported that the whole of Rodbourne Lane was in mourning on the Saturday afternoon of the funeral, blinds were drawn in every street, and shops in many places closed.

This lovely photograph, taken by George Stone the Swindon photographer, shows the Congregational Church at the junction of Bath Road and Victoria Road, *c.* 1900. Originally built in 1866, the church was demolished in 1949. To the left of the church can be seen Apsley House, presently used as the museum. George Stone's premises were at 25 Faringdon Street, New Swindon, later used by other Swindon photographers including John Tait, Arthur Banbury and Leonard Maylott. For another picture of the church see *Swindon in Old Photographs III*, p. 107.

Westcott Place Mission Hall, *c.* 1920. This was known locally as the 'Kipper Loft'. The hall was upstairs, with access via an exterior stairway. The nickname is thought to have been acquired when, before it was a place of worship, it was used by Billy Griffin to dry fish brought to New Swindon via the canal, which ran behind the building. The hall was started in 1904 by John Greenwood and Jack Hacker, the latter continuing to lead the mission (together with other helpers) through both world wars until 1951, when the work was transferred to the former Methodist Chapel at William Street. It is now part of the Westcott Motors forecourt.

The Friends Meeting House, Eastcott Hill, 1968, Originally built in 1901, it is still in use today, but much enlarged.

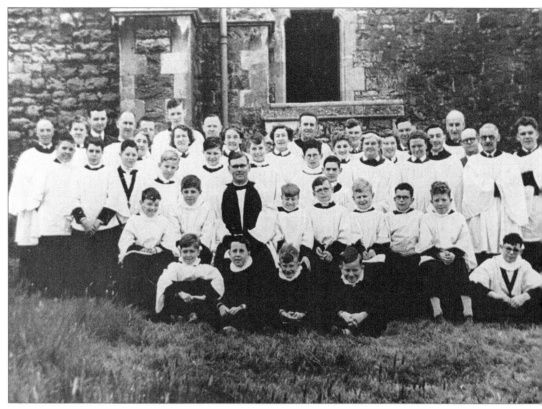

Christ Church Choir, 1956. Among the group is the curate, Glyn Calder, and the organist and choirmaster, Gordon Crabbe (who continued in this role until the end of 1995). Others identified include T. Key, B. Morgan, Mrs Brown, B. Cole, J. Maunders, R. Foord, Mrs Whitfield, S. Hedges, ? Tanner, D. Hobbs, Mrs Marsh, M. Williams, c. Morgan, ? Drinkwater, Mrs Herbert, Mrs. Taylor, A. Hayward, ? Ferrier, ? Holland, Miss Hughes, J. Stevens (who later became Mayor of Thamesdown in 1975), Mrs Jarvis, P. Little, Miss Young, B. Woods, H. Hobbs, Mrs Hayward, J. Cox, J. Stratford, R. Dunstan, N. Humphries, P. Edwards, D. Goodridge, M. Cook, ? Holland, ? Foster, ? Ferrier and B. Stratford.

Prospect Methodist Church, Prospect Place, 1968. The church was built in 1870 and subsequently enlarged by 1904. The building is now used by The Assemblies of the First Born Church, who have made considerable efforts in returning the interior to its former glory.

St Saviour's Church Drama Society, *c.* 1954. They were performing *Our Town*, by T. Wilder, which had been produced by Walter Priestley. Among those identified in the second row (sitting) are Barbara Whiting, Ken Berry, Nora Mantell, Joan Peddle, Olwen Nash and Brian Robinson.

The Regent Place Gospel Hall awaiting demolition, *c.* 1970. See *Swindon in Old Photographs III*, p. 103, and p. 88 of this book. The hall was situated behind the Savoy cinema (pictured at the rear of the building), and had opened on 25 December 1899, with special services being held the next day. The original membership of 54 grew eventually to 120, together with a well-attended Sunday school for the children. The building had been designed by William Hooper, the local photographer.

A view of one of Swindon's steepest streets, Prospect Hill, 1968. The boys are hauling their carts back up the slope for another race. The Rehoboth Baptist Church, on the left, has changed little except for a recently built new entrance (by the ladder in the photograph). The Beehive pub started life as an off-licence, before finally gaining a full licence in 1889. See also *Swindon in Old Photographs III*, p. 104.

Pictured are members of the Regent Hall Bible class on an outing to Charlton Ponds lake near Purton, August 1910. While on such events a picnic would be arranged along with boating and other activities, as well as fellowship issues. Among those identified on this William Hooper postcard are: (back row) William Dore, David Hacker, Mr Margetts, Henry Hacker; (third row) George Morse, Fanny Hacker, Mrs Hunt, Harry Flewellyn; (second row) Mrs Flewellyn, Mrs Dore, Joseph Dore, Lizzie Hacker; (front row) Will Morse, May Morse and the Margetts sisters.

Pupils of Walton House School, 1913. The school premises were at 10 Westlecott Road, and the man seated in the centre was the founder and headmaster, the Revd Harold Higgins. Formerly he was the curate at St Barnabas' Church, Gorse Hill, and in 1910 he started the school. Later, between the years 1933 and 1950, Mr Higgins was Rector of West Kington (near Chippenham). He died in 1953, aged 84.

Sanford Street School football team in the season 1922/3. Back row, left to right: A. Earthridge, G. Hobbs, J. Cockram; middle row: R. Brown, R. Broom, B. White, L. Pope; front row: D. Blount (master), L. Collier, J. Silto, F. Smith, R. Pike, B. Hunt, R. Bavin (Headmaster).

Clarence Street School football team, 1912/13 season. Back row, left to right: Dick Blount (also a famous football referee), Cliff Eatwell, Charlie Hinton, Andrew Morrison, Jimmy Ellison, Wally Winter, George Pressey; middle row: Eddie Everett, Arthur Bullock, Will Theobald, Sam Halestrap, Stan Hillier; front row: Arthur Knight, Arthur (Milky) Hillier and Fred (Scroggy) Shaw.

Commonweal Hockey Team, c. 1934/5. Back row, left to right: Miss Thompsett, Mary Collingbourne, Audrey Jones, Trixie Rickards, Cicely Cousins, Esme Elms, Miss Diffy; front row: Evelyn Farmer, Nina Collingbourne, Mary Greenhill (Captain), Barbara Whiting, Iris Coker.

The staff of Ferndale Road Junior School, August 1951. Back row, left to right: R.G. Row (Deputy Head), Miss S.M. Jones, Miss M. Howard (later to become Mrs Kemble), Mrs L. Dixon, R.T. Nash (Headmaster); front row: C.H. Gwyther, Miss N. Jervis, Miss P.L. Holmes (later to become Mrs Gilbert), G.A.L. Cussons.

CHAPTER SIX

WILLIAM HOOPER: MASTER PHOTOGRAPHER

A postcard from about 1910, showing that Hooper's shopfront was used as an advertisement to attract trade to his premises. On the reverse, potential customers were invited to have their portrait taken in the studio either in normal daylight or electric light. Hooper also claimed that he was acknowledged to be skilled in child portraiture, as well as specializing in bromide enlargements.

Pictured here are William and Mary Hooper,
c. 1910. The photograph was taken in the
studio of William's shop at 6 Cromwell Street,
which he retained until his retirement in 1921.

This beautiful period photograph shows William and Mary Hooper out and about on their tandem tricycle
in Swindon, c. 1897. William was famous for inserting his mode of transport in his photographs, whether
tricycles or, later, various motorbikes that he had purchased.

William Hooper, being a person with strong Christian convictions, often invited many of the visiting preachers who came to the church, to his home at Fairhaven. From time to time Pilgrim Gospel travellers called, such as on this occasion in about 1925. Pictured standing outside the caravan are, from left to right, Mrs Dunsford, Mary Hooper, Mr Dunsford, Peter Taylor and William Hooper.

A well-illuminated room at the photographic studio of William Hooper, c. 1910. This was used for developing the heavy glass plates which photographers used during this period. It is difficult to imagine the activity that would be needed in this room on occasions such as the tram crash, when Hooper had photographed the tram surrounded by the crowds (see *Swindon in Old Photographs I*, p. 99), brought the plates back, and developed and produced postcards for sale to the public by the next morning.

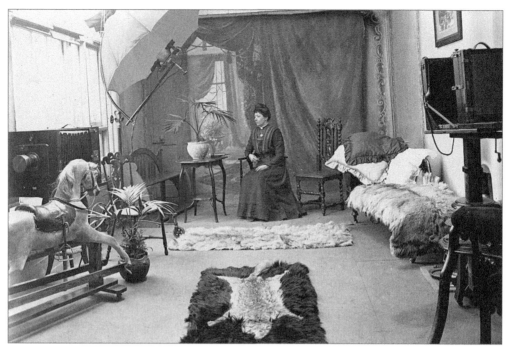

A most unusual view of the studio room at the Cromwell Street premises. It shows a spacious area with a variety of props for the different portraits he would offer. The rocking-horse would be used for slightly older children as opposed to the rug covering on the right which he used for infants. One of his elegant plate cameras is on display along with a serious-looking Mary sitting at the table.

Another view of the studio facilities within the premises at Cromwell Street, *c.* 1910, showing the portable cloth which was used as a backdrop for portraits, along with the flash unit and reflector (the umbrella). This is very similar to the type of equipment used by a modern photographer.

A view looking towards the doorway entrance of the roof garden from the main building in Cromwell Street, *c.* 1905. It looks very pleasant and peaceful for Leslie Richards and Mary sitting admiring the border display of flowers.

This photograph was obviously taken for the family album by William Hooper, *c.* 1908. It shows the roof garden they had built over the extension to the shop in Cromwell Street, which allowed opportunities (weather permitting) for relaxation. Mary is holding a dead mouse while the Hoopers' four cats are paying close attention to her every movement.

This rare photograph shows William Hooper alongside his telescope on his roof garden at Cromwell Street, and is titled 'How I photographed the eclipse'. This refers to the eclipse of the sun on 17 April 1912. It began at 10.15 a.m. and was closest to a total eclipse at 12.10 p.m., before being clear at 1.30 p.m. William obviously had the opportunity to combine two of his interests, astronomy and photography.

The finished result of William's efforts, produced on a postcard. This shows the stages of the eclipse at 11.20 a.m., 12.09 p.m. and finally 12.40 p.m.

William and Mary sitting proudly on their motorcycle and sidecar outside their Cromwell Street shop, c. 1912. Whenever time allowed they explored the small villages in the area, usually accompanied by William's camera equipment to record the scenes or local events.

Regent Hall, off Regent Street. This building was erected in 1899 as an Open Brethren meeting place and continued to be used by the Fellowship until 1967, when it was demolished in the redevelopment of the town centre. Pictured outside are, from left to right, Miss E. Hacker, Mary Hooper, Joseph Dore and Thomas Hacker.

William Hooper, while working as an apprentice in the GWR Works, came into contact with Joseph Dore. William was converted to Christianity as a result of listening to this man, and joined other believers at King Street Hall in 1883. As the numbers grew it became apparent that larger premises were needed. William, together with Joseph Dore, Thomas Hacker and Tom Richards, obtained a site with funds made available by fellow members. William took charge of the design and organizing of the construction of Regent Hall. It was from here that the Open Brethren Movement expanded and spread across the town and local area with halls in Florence Street, Kingsdown, Westcott Place (see p. 73), Pinehurst and Wroughton. Alice Stroud (Mary's sister) married Tom Richards, and this began the onset of a remarkable friendship between William and Tom which lasted until William's death in 1954. Tom Richards worked in the GWR workshops and offices until his retirement in 1932. His interests were astronomy, telescopes and microscopes, and his extraordinary skill at improving optical lenses and modifying microscopes helped William with the equipment he needed. Their combined interests resulted in the superb legacy of photographs which today still remain famed for their clarity. For another picture of the hall, see *Swindon in Old Photographs III*, p. 103, and p. 76 of this book.

A studio portrait by William Hooper of his friend Joseph Dore sitting with his grandchild, c. 1905. Joseph worked in the GWR Works for many years, and had been nicknamed 'Holy Joe' by his fellow workers. This was for his constant reading of the Bible, along with taking every opportunity of informing his workmates of their need for salvation through the Lord. Joseph Dore, who had become a charge-hand erector within the Works, died suddenly, early one morning at work, on 10 October 1913.

A portrait of Thomas Hacker, taken by his great friend William Hooper, shortly before he died on 30 October 1904, aged 69. See p. 44 for another picture of Thomas with his family. Thomas Hacker had been one of the early pioneers in Swindon of the Evangelistic Mission group, and helped in the dinner hour meetings at the GWR Works entrance as well as the old market in Emlyn Square. These meetings aroused great opposition at the time, and some of the speakers, including Hacker, were prosecuted. He framed his police court summons for 3 November 1881 – for standing bareheaded and preaching loudly in Princes Street, where the assembled crowd caused obstruction of the passages – and displayed it with pride as a testament to his beliefs. After a period of time the Mission group broke up in Swindon and Thomas instigated a meeting of twelve of the followers at a hall in Merton Street on 30 November 1899, which formed a church under the Open Brethren beliefs. For some time the family lived at Broad Hinton and Thomas took up farming. During this period he suffered serious injury while travelling in his trap. The horse bolted and as he tried to control it with the reins, he fell between the horse and trap. His head passed beneath the wheels of the trap and he was scalped. A doctor tended him and with assistance from Mary Hooper (wife of William) nursed him back to reasonable health, although he never regained his full former state. The family returned to Swindon and again chose to live in Merton Street, this time opening a haulage business. At his funeral in 1904 one of the hymns sung he had himself composed some nine months earlier, and it was also sung at his widow's funeral six years later.

The 'Trip' holidays always gave William Hooper a marvellous opportunity to photograph many of the Swindon families about to leave on their day-trip to the seaside. On this occasion, *c.* 1908, his wife Mary is pictured alongside No. 3424 *Sir N. Kingscote*, a William Dean-designed locomotive, which would be one of many lined up in the sidings on these occasions.

A studio portrait by William Hooper of his wife Mary, Leslie Richards and Alice Richards (Leslie's mother), *c.* 1913. Mary and Alice were sisters whose maiden name had been Stroud.

A family photograph taken in the late 1930s at Fairhaven, Upper Stratton. Back row: Tom Richards, Stanley Richards, William Hooper, Leslie Richards; front row: Grace Richards, Alice Richards, Mary Richards, Mary Hooper and Edna Richards.

William Hooper was born in the Cotswold village of Windrush in 1864. After school he worked for a time as a gamekeeper on the estate of Lord Sherborne. He left after an argument and came to Swindon in 1882 looking for employment, which he found in the GWR Works as an apprentice mechanic assistant in the 'B' Shop. At the age of 22 he lost part of his right leg in an accident with one of the traverses in the shop. After recovery, he resumed work for a few years before being forced to leave the Works on medical advice. In his spare time he had been a keen photographer and this was to become his means of employment. During his spell in the Works he met Joseph Dore, whose Christian testimony changed his whole outlook to life, and he retained from this period a strong Christian faith. On joining the Fellowship at King Street Hall, in time he befriended Mary Stroud, who became his wife in 1890 in a ceremony at the Baptist Tabernacle, Regent Circus. With the help of his wife Mary, his photographic business began in a room at 22 Merton Street, in the early 1890s, and progressed with the growth of the business first to 2 Market Street (in 1901–2), and in 1906 finally to 6 Cromwell Street where they remained until he retired in 1921. The business premises were bought by Fred Palmer who maintained the photographic tradition for many years. After his retirement he moved to Fairhaven at Upper Stratton, which allowed more time for his other interests of gardening, astronomy and painting. They remained here until the Second World War when they moved to 12 St Margaret's Road, Old Town. William Hooper died in 1954, aged 90.

A view up the drive towards their home at Fairhaven, Upper Stratton, *c.* 1930. The house was close to St Phillip's Church in an open area of Stratton. Close by were allotments where William rented one of the plots to grow vegetables.

This is thought to be one of the last photographs taken of William and Mary Hooper in 1954 when he was aged 90. Left to right: Tom Richards, Alice Richards, Mary Hooper, William Hooper and Grace Richards.

CHAPTER SEVEN

SPORT & ENTERTAINMENT

Swindon Rugby Club pictured at their Black Horse ground in the season 1932/3. Seated in the centre of the second row is Edward Twitcher, who was the club's founder. Members of the club at the time included many famous Swindon names, such as Pakeman, Toomer, Treasure, Wilmer, Dale, Hill, Silto and Nash.

The County Ground, *c.* 1920. In 1891 an area of 25 acres on the site of the present County Ground was obtained from the Goddard family. The cricket ground and pavilion (in background) was laid out/built in 1892/3 and the first game, Wiltshire v. MCC, was played there in 1894. Since 1895 it has been the home of Swindon Cricket Club, and many famous players and first class county teams have graced its turf.

The County Ground in the 1920s, with a large crowd in front of the Victorian pavilion watching a cricket match.

The Swindon Victoria Cricket Club, 1925. Back row, left to right: M. Hall, R.M. Rushan, D. Townsend; middle row: K. Taylor (Umpire), W. Phillips, C.R. Lainchbury, N. Litten, S.C. Taylor, *c.* Jones (Scorer); front row: E.M. Ferris (Vice-Captain), A.W.J. Peck (Hon. Sec.), Mr. T.C. Newman (President), F. Baldwin (Captain), H. Hanson; insets: F.W. Wheeler and F. Herbert.

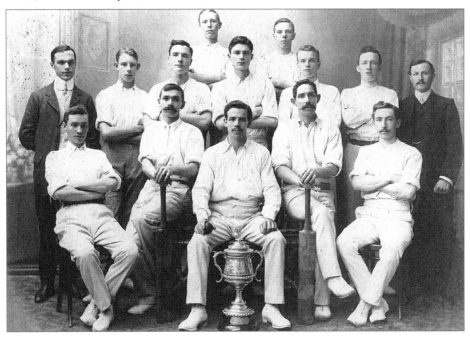

The Baptist Social Union Cricket Club, who had won the Swindon and District Amateur Cricket League in 1908. This photograph was taken by the Swindon photographers Protheroe & Simons. Back row, left to right: D. Townsend, R. Lainchbury; middle row: W. Greenwood, V.G. Williams, W.E. Roberts, F.C. Good, W. Scott, H. Hyland, *c.* Barrett; front row: *c.* Hyland, A.O. Turner, F. Baldwin (Captain), D. Hopkins, J.H. Gwyther (Sub-Captain).

Clifton Street Cricket Club, photographed in 1907 by William Hooper of Cromwell Street. They had just won the Swindon and District Amateur Cricket League. Back row, left to right: V. Crewe, A.T. Wilson (Scorer), F. Harvey; middle row: W. Hallewell, J. Nash (Umpire), E. Hallewell, R.E. Dodd, B.H. Gray, G. Morse, J. Gray (Vice President), *c.* Drewett; front row: F. Spreadbury, S.R. Gray (Captain), J. Clarke (President), F. Wheeler (Sub-Captain), W. Clarke.

Proudly showing the trophies they won in the 1930 season are the GWR Chief Mechanical Engineer's Office Cricket Team. They were winners of the 'All Line' Challenge Cup and the 'Plaister' Shield competitions. Back row, left to right: A.E.S. Fluck, J.C. Fido, E.C. Burden, A.W.J. Peck, E.F. Glastonbury, C.R. Lainchbury, E.S. Glastonbury; front row: H.P. Foulds, P.F. Pillinger, N.W. Litten (Captain), Mr. J. Kelynack, F. Holloway (Vice-Captain), M. Hall, G.H. Binnie; seated on the floor: R.W.H. Adlam, G.P. Tatley.

A fine portrait of HM Factory Tug of War 'A' team who won the Victoria Hospital Challenge Cup in 1920. Back row, left to right: P. Jefferies (Sec.), A.E. Beard (Treas.), J.C. Hall (Pres.), F. Ferris; middle row: S. Spackman, W. Spackman, T. Plumb (Capt.), G. Parker; front row: c. Mayo, G. Chaplin, J. Parry.

The Drill Hall, Church Place, *c.* 1933, with members of the Gymnasium Club watching a fencing demonstration. This club was run by Mr Crompton (pictured between the two fencers). They met once a week, and the joining fee was 2*s* 6*d*. The other man pictured is Jack Brown, the farthest fencer is Gwen Richens and the only other person identified is Ruby Watt, fourth from the left in the back row.

The Gymnasium Club again, *c.* 1933. Mr Crompton also ran a male section which put on displays in the GWR Park in the summer. The girls wore gymslips, which had to have strong elastic round the legs so as not to show the navy-blue knickers they wore!

Swindon Argyle Football Club, season 1921/2. The team played on St Mark's Recreation Ground, Whitehouse Road. This photograph of the team had been taken there on a Sunday, and when the Church authorities found out, it took a considerable amount of persuasion before the team was allowed to continue playing on the ground. Back row, left to right: S. Marshall, V. Telling (Vice-Captain), J. Fisher, R. Telling (Hon. Sec.), J. Parsons; middle row: E. Lay (Trainer), G. Webb, W. Bradfield, W. Lewis, E. Blizzard, E. Hall, E. Purbrick; front row: H. Blackford, F. Hill, W. Griffiths (Chairman), J. Smith (President), T. Hill (Captain), B. Holly, W. Crompton. The name of the mascot is unknown. Swindon photographer F. Humphrey took the photograph.

Swindon Wednesday United Football Club, 1923/4. Back row, left to right: D. Young, W. Woodman, W.A. Slade (Captain), Ginger Burgess, P. Ockwell; middle row: W.J. Dunmore (Hon. Sec.), J. Read, -?-, H. Burchell, A.E. Whatley (Trainer); front row: A.G. Stevens, E. Hayball, F. Sheppard, E.E. Hayball (Chairman), -?-, C.M. Hill, L. Hayball. The mascot in the front is W. Smith.

The Alfred Ridout Band, c. 1931. This had originally been called the St Mark's Church Band, as it started as a 'get together' for the church dance on a Saturday night and progressed from there. Identified are Alfred Ridout (the leader), Freddie Gore, Jack Thurow, Ted Smith; back row: Les Collier, Henry Bellinger, Norman Cook, Bert Ridout. Harry Smith, see *Swindon in Old Photographs V*, p. 118, played with the band for a period.

The Prospect Silver Band pictured outside the Town Hall, 1920s. At this time in Swindon there were several bands; these included the Swindon Town Military Band, Swindon Borough Military Band, Great Western (Swindon) Silver Band and the RAOB (Provincial Grand Lodge of England, Wiltshire Province). The Prospect had been founded in 1908 by Edward Bullock (when he was aged 17) and continued until 1948, two years after Edward's death. They were based at the Prospect Primitive Methodist Chapel. Although Edward worked in the GWR as a fitter and erector, most evenings were spent teaching local people to read music and play instruments. The members worked tirelessly to raise funds; these enabled silver instruments to be purchased along with the navy blue and gold uniforms. The band was a popular attraction at local fêtes, and they also headed the local hospital carnival procession for many years. Upon Edward's sudden death in 1946, his brother Robert led the band until it was disbanded. Edward's silver trumpet (a gift from his fellow bandsmen on his 21st birthday) is now on display at the Swindon museum. See p. 136 of this book showing the band leading the procession in 1940; also see *Swindon in Old Photographs V*, p. 33, for another view of the band at Emlyn Square.

Billy Richardson playing the part of Jack Point, a strolling jester in the Gilbert and Sullivan light opera *The Yeomen of the Guard*, March 1938. Besides appearing in many performances for the local musical societies, he was also a member of a concert party group called 'The Wags' which performed in the theatres. Billy also performed the role of compère at the show when the local Hospital Carnival Queen was selected. See also *Swindon in Old Photographs V*, p. 117.

'The Visitors' in the production of *The Toreador* performed by the Swindon Amateur Musical and Dramatic Society in February 1929. Left to right: Arthur Blackman, Phyllis Macpherson, Harold (Spud) Lowings, ? Reynolds, Charlie Macpherson, Marjorie Cheshire. See *Swindon in Old Photographs V* for later photographs of the Macphersons during their year of office as the Mayor and Mayoress of Swindon in 1944/5.

This photograph shows the cast of *The Toreadors* gathered on the stage of the Empire Theatre in 1929. The Society had been formed in 1922 to give operatic, dramatic and orchestral performances in the town, the proceeds of which were donated to charity.

John Prosser and his Rhythmic Revels, early 1930s. The line-up was Harry Smith, Charlie Comley, Bert Amor, John Prosser, Sid Pymm and Bill Sutton. See *Swindon in Old Photographs V*, p. 118, for a later band which involved Harry Smith as the leader.

The Johnnie Stiles Band, at the BBC Studios Bristol, Boxing Day, 1940. They were recording a session for 'Music While You Work'. Back row, left to right: Charlie Comley, Gordon Talbot, John (Jock) Walker, Roger Summerfield, Maurice Cole, Ron Richards; front row: Ronnie Grant, Peter Coleman, Arthur Marsh, Johnnie Stiles, Harry Smith, Jim Mason.

Pictured after winning their first ever Dance Band contest are the Johnnie Stiles Band. This win at Reading was the first of many and would eventually lead them to become the All-British Dance Band Champions in both 1948 and 1949. Back row, left to right: Les Taylor, Eric Goodman, Gordon Talbot, Arthur Marsh, Sam Morgan (the band's manager); front row: Pete Coleman, Phil Hillier, Charlie Comley, John (Jock) Walker, Johnnie Stiles, Ken Kitchen, Roger Summerfield.

Len Winslow and his New Sylvians Dance Band at the Bradford Hall (now called The Arts Centre), 1939. When originally formed it had been the New Sylvians Dance Band, see *Swindon in Old Photographs V*, p. 120. Later it became known as Bert Cullingford and his New Sylvians, but by this time Bert Cullingford had been seconded to the US Army for the war effort, and Len Winslow had taken over. Back row, left to right: Jack Bridgeman, Eddie Whatley, Len Winslow; front row: Maurice Cole, John (Jock) Walker, Frank Clarke, Roger Summerfield.

This photograph shows a section of the Gordon Talbot Orchestra playing at the McIlroys dance hall in 1963. Left to right: Joe McShane, Bernie Smith, Ronnie Grant and Roger Summerfield. See *Swindon in Old Photographs V* for further photographs of Roger Summerfield in Swindon bands.

The Harry Smith Band at Churchfield School for a charity dance in aid of hospital radio, 1970s. Harry had originally formed the band in 1935, when he had been manager of the Bradford Hall (now called the Devizes Road Art Centre). Back row, left to right: Joe Giles, Eddie Edwards, Ernie Fisher; front row: Trevor Matthews, Wally Chatfield, Harry Smith, Ken Smith, Frank Jeffcutt.

CHAPTER EIGHT

COMMUNITY LIFE,
LEISURE & HOLIDAYS

*This heavily decorated lorry belongs to Bown & Co., Lagos Street, who were mineral water manufacturers.
Among the carnival decorations can be seen the relevant message: 'So buy Bown's and keep Swindon men
employed'. The photograph was taken in the 1920s.*

Posing for the photographer on an outing are members of the Swindon Wheelers Bike Club, *c.* 1926. On this occasion they are visiting the Blowing Stone at Kingston Lisle, near Wantage. The only member so far identified is William (Bert) Slade on the extreme right.

The same group from Swindon Wheelers. The notice on the tree relates that 'any small contribution given by visitors using the key of the Blowing Stone will be given to the fund for supporting the village nurse. Visitors are requested to kindly enter the amount in the book kept for the purpose.'

Pictured at Coate Water, on Wednesday 6 September 1916, are Clara Ellen Brown (left) and Daisy Lovelock, who was her companion and housekeeper.

Members of the Percy Street Working Men's Club on an outing to Gough's Caves at Cheddar, 10 July 1922. The charabanc was licensed to carry twenty-eight passengers and it appears, from the photograph, that only one lady was present.

A Borough of Swindon bus at Salisbury while on a trip to Weymouth, 1926. Among the passengers are, at the rear of the bus, Charlie and Elsie Browning with Bert and Vera Shipton. During this period the myth started that all the Swindon bus drivers were called 'Dennis', after the nameplate on the front which, in reality, was the name of the bus manufacturer!

Posing for this photograph taken on the seafront at Brighton are ladies on a day trip from Compton's factory in Sheppard Street, *c.* 1937. From left to right: Violet Shipton, Floss Uzzle (who was the forewoman), Gwen ?, Gwen Curtis.

The 1st Swindon Boys' Brigade at summer camp, Lechlade, *c.* 1921. The boys had marched from Swindon to the camp, and would return the same way. Meetings were held at the Central Mission Hall, Regent Circus. Back row, left to right: Norman Fowler, Lt Chew, Superintendent Iles, Wesley Sage, Norman Carver; middle row: Ivor Richards, Norman Leighfield, Capt. Milne, Capt. Dawes, Cyril Smith; front row: Les Collier, Bert Witts, Charlie Dobson, Reg Cosway.

1st Swindon Girl Guides, outside Sanford Street Congregational Church Sunday School entrance, *c.* 1929–30. Barbara Whiting is fifth from the left in the back row; Fay Howard is fourth from the left in the middle row, with Miss Robinson (Captain) next to her and Olive Rollo on the extreme right; Hilda Vallance is third from the left in the front row.

This photograph illustrates very early Girl Guide uniforms, *c.* 1920. It shows the sisters Marion and Ada Channon from Wroughton who, along with Miss Drew, were founder members of 1st Wroughton Guides.

Pictured at the doorway to 23 Akers Way, Moredon on 15 November 1950 are Girl Guides Pat Reeves and Joan Bates. They are awaiting the arrival of Princess Elizabeth to view the newly built houses on her tour of the town. Pat Clark (née Reeves) has continued in the Guide movement and now holds the positions of District Commissioner of Swindon Central District, Brownie Guider and Assistant Guide Guider of Central Church, as well as being County Archivist.

Pictured outside the Empire Theatre, Groundwell Road, in bright sunlight are Guide leaders (from left to right) Gladys Loder, Hilda King, Joan Mitchell, Marjorie Holliday and Margaret (Skip) Gover.

Celebrations on the occasion of the twenty-first birthday of the 1st Swindon Guides, 1935. Miss Ceris Williams is cutting the cake, watched by the Guides.

A gathering of the past and present members of the 4th Caledonian Rangers to celebrate their twenty-first birthday party in 1959. The Rangers were formed at the Trinity Presbyterian Church in Victoria Road, and took the name from a request by the Scottish Minister, the Revd John Gavin, to use the Gordon tartan as the neck-tie. Among those present were 'Skip' Gover and 'Cap' Holiday (sitting in the centre). The front row includes Beryl Blackford, Pam Law, Merle Hawksbee and Angela Gray, while some of the others are Phyllis Mayfield, Clair Huck, Bet Johnson, Janet Longman, Janet Dudman and Paddy Tonge. The Rangers are the senior branch of the Girl Guides Association.

The opening of the Girl Guides' campsite (Elcombe) on land at Chilton Farm, Wroughton, 1951. Among the dignitaries at the opening ceremony were (from the left) the Vicar of Wroughton, Miss Marguerite De Beaumont (who officially opened the site), Mrs Ramsey, Mrs Mattingly, Miss Elmie Thorne, Miss Grainger and Miss Hilda King.

A meeting of local Girl Guides at the Planks, 1933.

The Town Gardens, July 1945, with the Mayoress (Mrs P. Macpherson), talking to some of the guests at the OAP Tea Party. Nearly 650 attended the event. It was reported that the oldest people present were Mr and Mrs S. Wiltshire of Lethbridge Road, aged 81 and 90 respectively.

Coate Water and children happily paddling in the pool, *c.* 1939, which is now converted into a sand-pit play area with numerous slides and swings. For the delights of paddling, parents now have to take their children to the converted swimming pool at the entrance side of the lake.

Walcot Boys' Club building, off Buckhurst Crescent, was visited by the well-known entertainer Frankie Vaughan on 9 May 1962. During the day he also visited Park South Boys' Club and Stratton St Margaret Hospital. He gave considerable time to the Boys' Club events throughout the country, promoting their ideals in gratitude for the time he spent as a youngster in a similar club in Leeds. The building has since been demolished and the Baileys Farm Gardens, flats for young single people, have been built in its place.

The Town Gardens, with children gathered round the pond watching the fountain, c. 1916. The pond has recently been returned to its original use after being filled in by the council in 1996 when it was unable to complete necessary repairs at the time. The water feature was restored in time for the 1997 *Old Town Festival*, helped by considerable pressure from local residents.

A group outing from the Rodbourne Road Working Men's Club to London to watch Swindon Town play at Loftus Road against Queens Park Rangers on 17 April 1971 (Swindon lost 4–1). They are pictured at the Royal Oak Hotel in Brent, London. Among those identified are Mervyn Hill, Ron Beaven, M. Hickey, T. Bauer, K. Lane, J. Stokes, Heinz (Harry) Kuna, G. Fitchett, G. Huckin, S. Williams, A. Ricks, F. Selwood (Steward of Morris Street Club), c. Birks, Den Turner, E. Watts, A. Davis, G. Huntley, A. Cheese, S. Turner, Mr Sarash, D. Hedges, J. Glover, P. Hinton, F. Hinton, B. Savory, P. Hedges, G. Kennett, A. Hillier, R. Read, R. Beale, M. Price, E. Morcott, F. Morse, P. Mitchell, P. Wootton, S. Ferris, L. Brown, T. Hickey, J. Litten, G. Trueman, J. Vane, Nobby Noble and D. Jenkins (Club Steward).

CHAPTER NINE

EVENTS & PEOPLE

The first visit of an aeroplane to Swindon, 27 July 1912. M. Salmet, the French pilot, is waiting for the field to be cleared for an exhibition flight. He had landed his aircraft at Pipers Corner, Coate Road. It was reported that there was a crowd of 30,000 to watch him perform a display of aerobatics! See also Swindon in Old Photographs I, *p. 116, and IV, p. 104.*

A rare occasion when the three Macpherson brothers were on leave together in 1918. This photograph, by the Swindon firm of Protheroe and Simons, shows John (Royal Flying Corps), Charles (South Lancs. Regiment) and George (unknown). Charles later became the Mayor of Swindon in 1944–5 (see *Swindon in Old Photographs V*, pp. 133, 140–4).

A procession passing the frontage of the Swindon Technical College, Victoria Road, 22 June 1911, during the Coronation celebrations for King George V and Queen Mary.

A very rare photograph which shows GWR men on strike in August 1911. They are pictured outside the Union Railway Hotel in Sheppard Street. The National Railway Strike lasted from 18 to 23 August, and the dispute had originally started in Liverpool on the Lancashire and Yorkshire Railway. The men had given notice to strike when the company immediately started employing 'blacklegs'. This had the effect of uniting, for the first time, the major railway unions and the resultant strike caused immediate difficulties throughout the country, including food shortages. Although there were only thirty men employed in the Swindon goods yards, elsewhere, such as in Bristol and Avonmouth, the numbers were nearer 700. At the same time strikes were also breaking out on the omnibuses in London, and the Prime Minister, Mr Asquith, was soon under considerable pressure. The *Evening Advertiser* called it 'a state of siege', and reported that prices had risen on what goods were available, such as meat. This all occurred during a period of very hot weather, with reports of the fire brigade attending several fires in the fields around Westlecot Road. This could explain the *Advertiser* reporting that 200 men had threatened to rush the GWR station. Investigation by union officials, and reported to the police, found not the slightest foundation for this report.

The strike ended on Saturday night (the 23rd), after talks between David Lloyd George and Sydney Buxton (Board of Trade), and the unions. In Swindon a meeting was held the next day in Princes Street recreation ground, and several thousand people attended. There were three improvised platforms erected for the speakers, who included Mr R.C. Lambert, the local MP, Mr Selwood, a goods fireman, who was Chairman of the Strike Committee and Mr Mayall, Secretary of the Swindon Branch of the ASRS. Mr Slade, Secretary of the Associated Enginemen's and Firemen's Society, thanked everyone for the support given to the men. Mention was made especially of the women, who helped with the supply of tea and cocoa to the pickets during the nights. The speakers also reported that it had been a clean fight in the town except for the lies in the *Advertiser* relating to the alleged threat on the part of the strikers to rush the station premises. This would appear to be very frank newspaper reporting by the *Advertiser*! In the early period of its history the Union Railway Hotel was known as the GWR House, and would open at 6.00 a.m. selling hot coffee with a tot of rum to the workers. It finally closed in 1958 and was purchased by Comptons to extend their premises.

Crowds line the route to the Town Hall on the occasion of the royal visit of King George V and Queen Mary to the town on 28 April 1924. See *Swindon in Old Photographs II*, pp. 79 and 118, for other crowd scenes of the same visit.

This photograph shows children patiently waiting in Faringdon Road on 28 April 1924 during the visit to the town of King George V and Queen Mary. The children attended Jennings Street School and had been brought by their teachers Miss Matthews (left of centre) and Miss Potter (right) to catch a glimpse of the royal couple on their way to the GWR Works. Among the children are Ted Hazell, Ron Critchley, Hilda Stevens, Rose Loveday, Frances Barnes, Nellie Jackson, Vera Walters, Les Munro, Les Cowley, Ron de Turkerville, Betty Smart, Jim Mulcock, Arthur Neate, Percy Norris, Les Clapham and Walter Turk.

Pictured in the back garden of their home in Page Street are the Ireland family, *c.* 1910. From the left are Charles, Jonas, May, Harold, Gladys, Susan and Albert. Charles, whose actual Christian names were Walter Charles Jonas, started work in 1909 with William Hooper, the Swindon photographer, and later started an apprenticeship with him on 24 February 1910. Unfortunately this was not completed, because of the death of his father and the fact that he was the eldest son, which resulted in him seeking better paid employment to support the family.

Victor Hemming, aged 2, with his whip and toy horse, 1910. He was born at the Crown public house, 2 Marlborough Road (until recently the site of Gilberts showroom). At birth he weighed only 2 lb, and was said to have been put in a pint mug on the bar. The Crown in later years had a reputation for disreputable clientele and was suddenly closed in 1955 to enable the licence to be transferred to the Oddfellows Arms. At the time of closure it was the only thatched pub remaining in Swindon.

Pictured here is Ivy Sexton (centre), who has just been elected Swindon's Carnival Queen at the Drill Hall on 10 June 1935. She is surrounded by her attendants: Kathleen Luxton, Jessie Cullingford, Doris Smith, Elsie Wilks and Dora Fricker. Ivy who lived in Manchester Road, was crowned by Mr Freddie Fox (winning jockey of the Derby), who had ridden six races at Wolverhampton before travelling down for the event. At the Grand Concert which followed, entertainment was supplied by Olive Wilks (contralto), Raymond Hatherall (tenor), Harry Thomson (magician and entertainer), Arthur J. Love (piano accordion) and the Swindon Symphony Orchestra, conducted by Edgar P. Monk.

The main sign being erected at the entrance to Coate Water, Marlborough Road, in June 1948, advertising the main facilities of bathing, boating, fishing and teas, along with the fact that it had been the home of Richard Jefferies, the local author. Two of the men involved were Jim Smith, a carpenter (centre), and the blacksmith Bert Shipton (right).

Pictured here at the council yard in Cromwell Street in 1945 is blacksmith Bert Shipton. The council were still using a number of horses at this time. Among the jobs for Bert Shipton during the Second World War was the cutting down of the Faringdon Road park fences for the war effort. After the hostilities had ended he then had the task of making replacement fences.

Swindon-born Ralph Bates (centre) in Spain during the Civil War, 1937. Born in 1899, he went to work in the GWR factory from the age of 16, before enlisting in the 16th Queen's Royal West Surreys, serving in France as a private soldier until the end of the First World War; he then returned to Swindon and the GWR Works. A man of enormous energy, he is remembered for his exploits on Saturday mornings in the 'O' Shop (the Tool Room), of climbing up the drive belts and control shafts of the machines after they were turned off for the weekend, to the overhead roof struts, before crawling along from strut to strut across the shop and returning to the floor level on the other side. Always adventurous, he went to live in Spain in the 1920s, firstly at the docks in Barcelona and then as a travelling mechanic, fixing anything from village church organs to electrical systems. He lived mainly in the Pyrenees and became a skilled mountaineer. Ralph made his name as an author in the 1930s, with the novels *Sierra* (1933), *Lean Men* (1935) and, the most famous, *The Olive Field* (1936). The latter was published on the eve of the Civil War in Spain and he served at the front from the very beginning, helping to organize the International Brigade, of which he was a commissar, and editing their journal, *Volunteer for Liberty*. After the victory of the rebel forces under General Franco, Ralph escaped from Spain and went to live in Mexico and the USA. He continued his literary career and became Professor of Literature at New York University in 1948–68, then retired to Naxos in the Aegean. He divided his time between Naxos and his apartment in New York, where up to the end of 1996 he still replied to letters, although suffering from failing sight.

Pictured at their home at 17 Regent Place in 1946 are Grace and Richard Loveridge with Douglas, their grandson, aged 4. The house, long since demolished, was approximately in the position of the present-day Wyvern Theatre stage door.

Swindon Junction station with Princess Elizabeth having arrived on a visit to the town, 15 November 1950. The visit was to officially open the town's Garden of Remembrance and the Moredon Playing Fields. This was the first royal visit to Swindon since the early days of the Second World War, when King George VI and Queen Elizabeth paid unofficial visits, which newspapers would report as a royal visit 'somewhere in Southern England'.

Princess Elizabeth visiting the newly opened council houses in Akers Way, Moredon, 15 November 1950.
She was welcomed by Mrs Willmott at her home at 22 Akers Way.

Princess Elizabeth walking through the excited and smiling crowds in Leicester Street on her way from the Civic Offices to open the Garden of Remembrance, Swindon's War Memorial, on 15 November 1950. On the Princess's left is the Mayor, Ald. J. Bond. Also in the group are the Duke of Somerset (Lord Lieutenant of Wiltshire), the Mayoress (Mrs J. Bond), the Town Clerk (Mr D. Murray John) and Swindon's MP, Tom Reid.

The Garden of Remembrance, Groundwell Road, on the visit of Princess Elizabeth to officially open the garden on 15 November 1950. This was also the Golden Jubilee Year of the Borough and the event is recorded on the plaque just inside the gateway. The land and lake south of the garden were subsequently laid out using funds for Coronation celebrations in 1953 and the whole area renamed Queen's Park. In August 1997 two new plaques were dedicated and placed close to the originals.

Headlands Grove, at the junction with Cricklade Road, decorated with banners and bunting for the Coronation celebrations held there on 2 June 1953. On the left are the playing fields of Headlands Grammar School, which had been built in 1952. Among the events were a fancy dress parade for the children, shows of garden produce and a cake competition, and sports races (for under 5s up to 17 for children, then ladies and 'veterans' – men! There was also a comic football match (ladies v. men, dressed as the opposite sex), an ankle competition for ladies, knobbly knees for men and then dancing. As it was impossible to hire cutlery during this period, a request was made for people to bring their own knives, forks and spoons for the tea provided, which consisted of cold meat, salads, cakes and ices.

The Queens Park, June 1977, showing the floral display created by the council gardeners for the Silver Jubilee of Queen Elizabeth II.

CHAPTER TEN

SWINDON AT WAR

Old Town (Swindon Town) railway station on 23 April 1945, with the Mayor and Mayoress, Ald. and Mrs C.S. Macpherson bidding farewell to Col. Hewitt-Robinson of the US Army, when he and his troops departed from the station.

Victoria Road, Old Town, March 1944. Pictured is a mobile kitchen vehicle belonging to A Division of the National Fire Service, whose station was in Cromwell Street.

A mobile canteen trailer which had been presented to the National Fire Service in Swindon on 10 June 1944 by the Canadian Red Cross. The sign on the side shows that a Mr and Mrs A. Bronfman from Montreal in Canada had paid for the trailer.

Devizes Road, Old Town, 7 September 1939. Members of Station D of the Auxiliary Fire Service busy constructing an air raid shelter on the corner with Britannia Place. The men were C.G. Collier, J.W. Tod, L. Carter and J. Shakespeare.

The shopfront of Great Western Clothiers, 35–7 Faringdon Road, 1940s. This photograph shows the wartime shutters in place. It was the task of Dennis Morris (the apprentice, who later became the owner) to put the shutters in place, but it took so long that usually the all-clear sounded before he completed the job. The sign for Aquatite coats was the largest illuminated sign in the town at this time.

Victoria Road on the morning of 16 June 1940. The parade had started from the Town Hall and was headed by the Mayor of Swindon (Cllr H.R. Hustings). It included members of the AFS (Auxiliary Fire Service), St John Ambulance, Red Cross, ARP Services, ex-Servicemen, Sea Cadets and the Boy Scouts and was led by the Swindon Prospect Silver Band. They were marching to the Town Gardens for a service to mark the start of that year's Hospital Carnival Week. The actual service was lead by the Rural Dean (the Revd Eric Smith) with prayers offered by the Revd G.R. Blake. Shops in the background include John Carter, the wholesale and retail tobacco shop; next door was E.B. Letso (No. 97), the gentlemen's hairdressing establishment. For additional pictures of Prospect Silver Band see p. 101, and *Swindon in Old Photographs V*, p. 33.

The Town Gardens on 16 June 1940, during the Sunday Service at the Dome, which had opened in 1936. This service started the Hospital Carnival Week, when events took place to raise funds for Victoria Hospital. The Bishop of Malmesbury (Dr Ronald Ramsey) made an address appealing for funds.

The new Leyland motor pump which had just been supplied to the Swindon Fire Brigade, photographed at the fire station in Cromwell Street, November 1939.

Wellington Street, looking towards the garage and the Railway Mission on the corner. The date is 11 October 1939, and the funeral procession is for Mr Reginald Waite of Poulton Street. He had worked for the East Street Co-operative Society as well as being an officer in the Auxiliary Fire Service (C section) and a prominent member of the Railway Mission. The service took place at the Railway Mission with the bearers being shared between the Mission Sunday school teachers and serving firemen (six of each), with the service being taken by Mr E.M. Laurie. The photograph shows nearly sixty members of Swindon Auxilliary Fire Service leading the fire engine and cortège away from the Railway Mission past the Wellington Garage on its way to the Whitworth Road cemetery. Mr Waite had been secretary of the Young Peoples' Fellowship, as well as a former Sunday school teacher.

Devizes Road, Old Town, March 1944. A Swindon Corporation bus (No. 10) needs the attendance of the fire brigade. In the background is the newsagent and tobacconist, W.J. Champion, with its signs for 'Players Please' and 'Wills Gold Flake'. Next door is the sign for J.F. Boalch, butcher.

Devizes Road, Old Town again, with the fire brigade still attempting to control the smoke coming from the Corporation bus. Unfortunately it will not reach Moredon, the destination advertised on the front. The bus certainly appears to have stopped all the traffic that day!

Pictured outside their station at Byron Street in 1945 are members of the AFS, sitting on their Dennis Standard T Country Appliance. Unfortunately we are unable to identify any of these men.

Members of the Swindon AFS (Auxiliary Fire Service) standing around their Standard T Heavy Unit lorry, Byron Street, 1944. This was one of several sites within the town which were used for the AFS men.

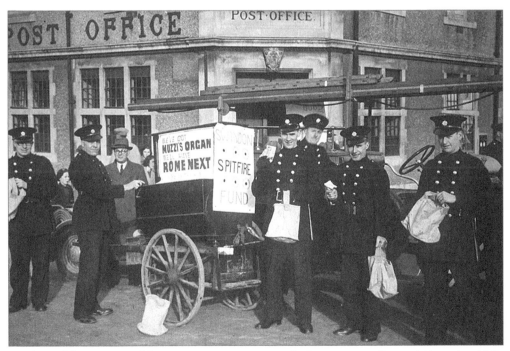

Members of the D Station of the AFS at Regent Circus outside the main post office on 8 November 1940, busily collecting for the Swindon Spitfire Fund. Written on the side of the organ is the slogan 'We've got Muzzi's Organ – we'll have Rome next – it's up to you.' The men are E. Shorter, P. Wheatley, L. Wright, R. Stephen, H. Compton, F. Adams, J. Tod and E. Hawkins.

Avenue Road, Old Town, *c.* 1940, showing the dismantling of garden railings. For many years afterwards small metal stumps could be seen on the walls around the town – relics from supplying metal to help in the war effort.

Group of schoolchildren pictured on the corner of Northampton Street outside no. 26, *c.* 1940. The children are, from the left, David Lacey, Donald Evans, Keith Tucker, Brenda Matthews, Patricia Burton, Josie Adams and Pat Dolan. The bicycle leaning against the wall belonged to Albert Beaney, see *Swindon in Old Photographs V*, p. 123.

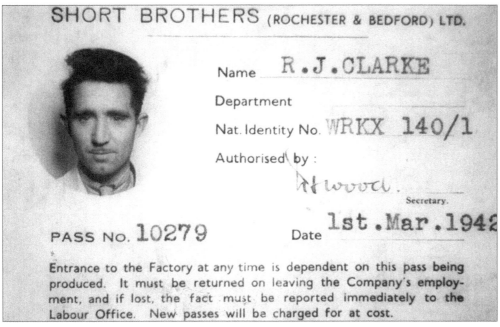

The pass that was required to gain entry to the Short Bros buildings on the GWR site during the Second World War. Short Bros' entrance was at the slope (later known as Shorts' Hill by locals) on the edge of Ferndale Road recreation ground and Osborne Street, now part of the Oasis traffic island. Mr R.J. Clarke worked there as an inspector on the parts produced for aircraft.

The Mayor of Swindon, Ald. C.S. Macpherson, opening the exhibition of toys at the Town Hall, 1 December 1944. They were made by local organizations for distribution to the orphans and needy children of the borough at Christmas time. Also in the picture are Divisional Officer Philpotts (NFS), Fred Titcombe (Mayor's mace bearer), Dr Roberts (Medical Officer of Health) and Mrs Macpherson (Mayoress).

Florence Street, Gorse Hill during the VE celebrations, 1945. J. Patey, the wood merchant, is supplying pony rides to the local children. Among those identified are Patrick Freeguard (Whiteman Street), Roy Dixon (Florence Street), Ian and Graham McDeson (Florence Street), Jill Porter (Suffolk Street).

Residents of the houses in Brooklands Avenue and Harvey Grove during celebrations on VJ Day, 1945.

CHAPTER ELEVEN

THE CHANGING FACE OF SWINDON

An 'Old Firm' bus pictured at their Swindon terminus in Temple Street, outside the gas showrooms, c. 1953. The Hawkins family, from High Street, Wroughton, ran a service from Wroughton to Swindon until July 1955, when the Bristol Omnibus Company purchased the contract to take over the route. See also Swindon in Old Photographs II, pp. 71–2.

A view along Drove Road from the junction with Southampton Street, *c.* 1935. The photographer stood in front of the Oxford Hotel (recently opened in 1929) to take the picture. The open ground on the left would become the site of the Drove Road school complex.

The houses in Medgbury Road, 18 April 1962, shortly before they were demolished. These houses backed on to the old canal in the approximate position of Cockram Court today.

Regent Street with Edgeware Road on the left, early 1950s. The shopfront of Woodhouse and Son advertises 'no deposits' and 'see our part exchange offers' in a bid to generate business. Next door in Regent Street is True Form, who advertised themselves as 'expert shoemakers'.

Hinders store, 115–18 Commercial Road, 1968. The shop sold everything from pets and fish to all garden requirements. A new office block, Anglia House, now stands on this site on the corner with Temple Street, with Taylors, estate agents, and Terry Warner, sports equipment, on the ground floor. See *Swindon in Old Photographs I*, p. 110, for another view of the shop.

Looking towards Havelock Street, 1968, with a narrow back-way leading to Granville Street. The shop on the right, Frank Woodward, fishing tackle shop, is now occupied by Cârlson Worldchoice, travel agents. The narrow back-way has now been widened as an access route from the car park into Havelock Street. Iceland's store, Havelock Square, now stands on the site of the bookshop and café in this picture.

The Westcott Free Off-Licence and Stores, 23 Westcott Place, 1968. It must have been a hot day when the photograph was taken – see the boy drinking from the bottle, while his friends await their share. Notice also the Moulton bicycle in the foreground.

Shops in Fleet Street, 1968: Kane's cycle and mopeds at 37–8, and The Kandy Box at 39. In the background the construction of the AUEW building (Alexander House) is under way. Part of the old cycle shop is now occupied by Pasha's nightclub.

The new Divisional Police Headquarters under construction in Princes Street, 1968. Notice the young boy on his rather ancient delivery bicycle. This new building is now called Meredith House. For a view of the original Princes Street houses just prior to demolition, see *Swindon in Old Photographs V*, pp. 152 and 154.

Regent Circus looking towards the extension to the college, *c.* 1962. On the right can be seen the Bristol bus office on the corner of Rolleston Street. The building on the left is the showrooms of Islington Furnishing Co., the 'Modern Furnishers', now the site of Rudi's Bar. Notice the Morris Minor turning into Victoria Road, and the Ford Anglia outside the furniture shop.

The Fairy Castle mural, Westcott Place, 1976. This was a Bavarian castle landscape completed by Thamesdown Community Arts project. Now sadly gone, it was a reminder of the period when wall murals around the town added considerable colour to the streets.

The frontage of Duck, Son & Pinker, Milford Street, 1960s. The shop sold musical instruments, sheet music and records. Long established in the town, and previously at 9 Fleet Street, the company is now situated on the corner of Bridge Street and Fleet Street.

Milford Street from its junction with Fleming Way, looking towards Wellington Street, 1968. To the left, on the corner of Cheltenham Street, is Beale's café, famous as a meeting place for youngsters since the Second World War. At this time it was the meeting place for Mods as opposed to GIs in the war. Duck, Son & Pinker's music shop can be seen in the distance.

Drove Road/County Ground traffic island, 1966. The Swindon Town football ground is in the background with the now-demolished Shrivenham Road stand. Today the 'Magic Roundabout' complex of mini-islands has taken the place of the island, while the new stand has risen on the site of the old original Aldershot Tattoo stand, which had become the football stand when it was re-erected in Shrivenham Road. Originally named the Intel Stand, it is now called the South Stand.

The site of the Rendell's housing development taking shape at Toothill, May 1977. The estate of Toothill and therefore the development of West Swindon was officially opened on Thursday 8 April 1976, when the Minister of Housing and Construction, Mr Reginald Freeson, opened the first stage of the urban village at Markenfield.

Bradley's housing estate at Glebe Park with the Toothill cottages again, 1980. Small sections of the original A420 road may still be traced today in Freshbrook Way, with the original cottages surrounded by the modern houses of the new estates.

Building work surrounding the Toothill cottages on the old A420 road to Wootton Bassett, August 1978. This expansion would involve an area of 600 acres being used for housing, industrial and commercial activity, a district centre, schools and allocated open spaces.

A thought hard to imagine today, but this is the end of the M4 motorway in October 1971. Junction 15 was as far as the road had reached over this section.

Les Holland putting the finishing touches to his artwork on a mural at the site of Swindon Town station on the railway path/cycle way (the former railway track) to Rushey Platt, west Swindon, in September 1986. This celebrated the old MSWJR, whose locomotives were painted in a dark red livery, a colour scheme that must have presented a complete contrast to the livery of the GWR engines for Swindonians during the early years of the century. The mural, unfortunately, suffered through vandalism and has been replaced with a new painting in recent years.

An aerial view, looking across the developing site of the Burmah Oil Ltd office complex, April 1972. What can be seen quite clearly is the trackbed of the old MSWJR line running behind the gardens of the houses in Broome Manor Lane.

This picture shows the topping-out ceremony of the new offices which had been built for Burmah Oil, off Marlborough Road, 17 November 1972. Nicholas Williams, Managing Director of the Burmah Oil Company Ltd, has the honour.

ACKNOWLEDGEMENTS

The Swindon Society would like to thank all those who contributed to the compilation of this book, especially Society members Brian Bridgeman and David Bedford, who put the book together and selected the photographs to be used. Thanks are also due to David Bedford, Denis Bird, Colin Herbert and Paul Williams for providing many of the photographs used in the book.

Especial thanks are due to Pat Clark, Richard and Lydia Clarke, John Hacker, Mervyn Hill, John Ireland, Mrs Phyllis Macpherson, John and Sheila Povey, Bob Richards, Ken Selby, Derek and Gwen Shipton, and Roger Summerfield for supplying several photographs used herein and much information.

Our gratitude also goes to the staff of Swindon Reference Library, Burmah Castrol plc, Deacon & Son (Swindon) Ltd, Newsquest (Wiltshire) Ltd, W.H. Smith and Wiltshire Police for their help and assistance. For individual contributions and assistance the Society would like to thank:

Mrs J. Allen • Mr A. Beaney • Mr D. Bedford • Mr R. Bell • Mr E. Bender • Mrs A. Billingham Mr D. Bird • Mr E. Bizley • Mr B. Bridgeman • Mr A. Brown • Mr W. Butler Mrs P. Clark • Mr & Mrs R. Clarke • the late Mr D. Cole MBE • Mr G. Crabbe • Mrs M. Crews • Mrs C. Davis Mr A. Duke • Mr E. Fisher • Mrs M. Fishlock • Mr F. Foord • Mr M. Franklin • Mrs J. Greenaway • Mr C. Gwyther • Mr J. Hacker • Mrs K. Hemming • Mr & Mrs C. Herbert Mr D. Hicks • Mr M. Hill • Mr J. Ireland • Mrs S. Jackson • Mr D. Lacey Mr D. Luker • Mrs B. MacDonald • Mrs P. Macpherson • Mr D. Marchant • Mr D. Morris • Mr D. Pennycook Mr & Mrs J. Povey • Mr R. Richards • Mr T. Sarbaugh • Mr K. Selby Mr & Mrs D. Shipton Mr D. Skeates • Mr R. Skull • Mr J. Slade • Mrs S. Spackman • Mr R. Summerfield • Mrs M. Titcombe • Mrs E. Tod • the late Mrs E. Townsend • Mr W. Turk • Mr B. Walker Mrs R. Watt • Mrs B. Whiting • Mr P. Williams • Mr G. Young

Some doubts exist regarding the original source of some of the photographs used in this book and the Swindon Society apologizes for any omissions from the acknowledgements shown above. The Society would also welcome any comments or additional information regarding the photographs in this book or in the previous five volumes. Please contact Brian Bridgeman, Publicity Officer, Swindon Society, 69 Sandringham Road, Swindon, Wiltshire SN3 1HT, or David Bedford, 21 Elmore, Eldene, Swindon, Wiltshire SN3 3TL.

The Swindon Album, which was published in September 1997, has an error on the back cover for the photograph of the Town Hall. It should read: 'Town Hall, *c.* 1908. Originally opened on 2 October 1891 by the Marquis of Bath.'

Visit our website and discover thousands of other History Press books.

www.thehistorypress.co.uk